Guernsey
Alderney
Sark & Herm

David Greenwood

id Greenwood, an educationalist and writer on boating and marine matters, made his
ne in the Channel Islands in 1991 and has spent subsequent years exploring them and
lling their virtues to a wide readership through articles in travel and yachting journals.
is a regular contributor to *En Voyage* the inflight magazine of Aurigny Air Services (the
nnel Islands 'National' airline) and his work has also been published in *Practical Boat Owner*
a   *Yachting Monthly*. His boat 'Seaward Lady' can often be seen in any bay where there is a pub
v   in reasonable walking distance – if you spot her, climb aboard and say hello, you can
b   ssured of a warm welcome!

The Horizon Press

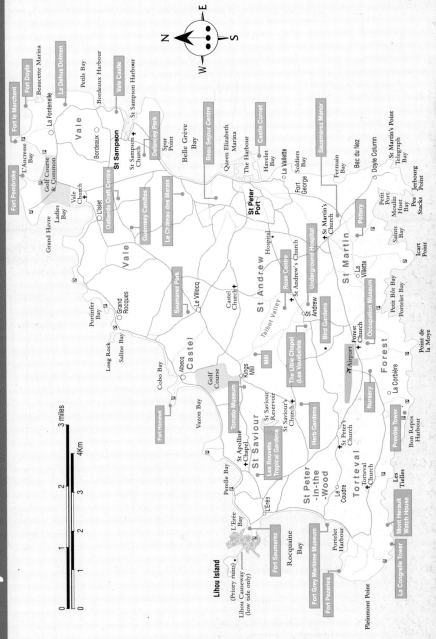

Guernsey

Fort le Marchant

Fort Doyle

Le Dehus Dolmen

Beaucette Marina

La Fontenelle

Petils Bay

Bordeaux Harbour

Vale Castle

St Sampson Harbour

Fort Pembroke

L'Ancresse Bay

Vale

Bordeaux

St Sampson

Spur Point

Belle Grève Bay

Delancey Park

St Sampson Church

Beau Sejour Centre

Queen Elizabeth Marina

Castle Cornet

Sausmarez Manor

St Martin's Point

Golf Course & Common

Ladies Bay

U'Islet

Vale Church

The Harbour

Havelet Bay

La Vallette

Soldiers Bay

Doyle Column

Telegraph Bay

Grand Havre

Oatlands Craft Centre

St Peter Port

Fort George

Fermain Bay

Bec du Nez

Guernsey Candles

Le Château des Marais

Vale

Portinfer Bay

Grand Rocques

Saumarez Park

Le Villocq

Castel Church

Hospital

St Andrew

Rosa Centre

St Andrew's Church

Underground Hospital

St Martin's Church

St Martin

Pottery

Petit Port

Moulin Huet Bay

Pea Stacks

Saints Bay

Icart Point

Long Rock

Saline Bay

Cobo Bay

Albecq

Castel

Golf Course

Kings Mill

Talbot Valley

St Andrew

Bird Gardens

Forest Church

La Villette

Occupation Museum

Petit Bôt Bay

Porlelet Bay

Point de la Moye

Fort Hommet

Vazon Bay

Tomato Museum

Mill

The Little Chapel (Les Vauxbelets)

Airport

Forest

Nursery

La Corbière

St Apolline Chapel

St Saviour

Les Rouvets Tropical Gardens

St Saviour's Reservoir

St Saviour's Church

Herb Gardens

St Peter's Church

Prévôte Tower

Bon Repos Harbour

Perelle Bay

L'Erée

St Peter -in-the -Wood

Le Coudre

Torteval Church

Torteval

Les Tielles

Mont Herault Watch House

Lihou Island

(Priory ruins)

L'Erée Bay

Rocquaine Bay

Porlelet Harbour

La Congrelle Tower

Fort Saumarez

Fort Grey Maritime Museum

Fort Pezeries

Lihou Causeway (low tide only)

Pleinmont Point

0   1   2   3 miles

0   1   2   3   4Km

Contents

Cruises around...

Feature Boxes

1. Welcome to the Channel Islands

About this book

This book is about a special place and a special people, a cluster of islands and their inhabitants who had the intelligence and strength of character to retain their identities and preserve their independence through countless years of conflict and rivalry between their neighbours. The Channel Island communities have had the foresight to be selective in their utilisation of twentieth century developments, placing the preservation of beauty and the natural environment above short term gain.

There is no place on earth like the Channel Islands, and to appreciate their full splendour

Guernsey Farm House

Top Tips

Guernsey

If you intend going to a beach, use the 'Which Bay' maps on pp 30-31.

Walk part of the coastal cliff path in the south or a circular walk out of Piedmont.

Take a trip to Alderney (fly), Herm & Sark (boat).

Visit Victor Hugo's House, Saumarez Park and Castle Cornet.

Try the bus tour around the Island, at 60p it has to be the best deal on Guernsey.

Herm

If time permits take the cliff path around the island and visit Shell Beach in the north.

Sark

Hire a bike or take a horse drawn taxi.

Visit The Seigneurie & Little Sark.

Alderney

Hire a car & explore the island or hire a bike.

and diversity, the islands of the Bailiwick of Guernsey should be your first ports of call.

In preparing this book, the author has visited all the islands on several occasions and his explorations were undertaken on bicycle and on foot. In Guernsey he travelled from St Peter Port in an anti-clockwise direction, because the hills are less severe that way. The chapters on Guernsey retrace his steps parish by parish.

Throughout the book he has attempted to describe the Islands and the people as they are now. Things change however, and so, to some extent at least, every visitor's journey must be an exploration.

Island magic

What is it about islands that they hold such special places in our imagination? Is it the childhood romance of marooned sailors, smugglers' caves, and pirate gold; or as adults, do we find reassurance in the easy definition that their shores provide? With islands there are no 'blurred edges'. The map has a reassuring perimeter of blue surrounding it. There are no roads leading over the edge and no questions unanswered. Maybe they fulfil a basic human need to compartmentalise our knowledge and understanding.

On an island it seems as if all the information required is available, contained within the irregular blue frame, so it appears understandable and attainable. In a confusing and ever changing world where 'absolute' truths are rare and usually obscure, islands offer a return to simple knowledge on a human scale.

Be careful though, islands are more than just passive rocks standing out of a featureless sea. They have strong magic and few people are unmoved by the experience of them. Stroll out to that high rock in the middle of the bay and wait for the incoming tide to surround it. You may have ten minutes to 'explore' your island before the sea imprisons you there.

Alternatively, watch a falling tide uncovering an offshore reef and tell me you haven't wanted to swim out to it. For just for a brief moment before the sea reclaims her, you can have sole jurisdiction. You can be alone and free to take possession of the cracks and crevasses, the high points and the secret places.

Therein lies the fascination of islands: isolated places, havens of safety for fleeing kings and exiles, yet at the same time, prisons for deposed emperors. Unlike any other destination your experience of them will depend upon your preparation and mode of arrival – read on, the magic starts here!

Why the Channel Islands?

These Islands are special. In the summer you can expect good weather and light clothes will usually be all you need, but take a jacket and some waterproofs for cooler evenings just in case. If you are looking for a beach holiday, the weather will be better than the UK. You can expect long sunny periods throughout the summer but it would be a shame to restrict your activity simply to sunbathing. There are a great deal of other things to do and see.

English money is acceptable. Access by

air or sea is relatively easy. There is a wide range of accommodation to suit every taste and pocket and the islands are clean, safe, and welcoming. What more could you wish for? Don't hesitate!

All the Islands in the Channel Island group have much in common. They are blessed with a climate considerably better than that of the UK, and in summer they're surrounded by a sea of clear emerald green and turquoise. Their shores are some of the cleanest in Europe and their granite cliffs offer some of the most beautiful and dramatic scenery to be found anywhere. They are famed for the beauty of their countryside and the excellence of their local produce – early potatoes, tomatoes, and rich cream from unique herds. If you enjoy good food, you'll discover restaurants here used to meeting the requirements of a sophisticated and discerning local clientele. Fish and shellfish could not be fresher. They're bought direct from the boats and served to customers only hours after being caught.

The Islands offer a wide range of activities – golf, fishing, sailing, swimming, sailboarding, surfing and diving. For historians and archaeologists there are examples of earthworks, architecture, and defences, from the Iron Age to the time of the German occupation in 1940. The military history of the Channel Islands is so rich that you'll find it at almost every corner. Even ordinary holidaymakers can catch the history bug. There is plenty here for World War II enthusiasts too. The German defence works in the Channel Islands are the best preserved of the entire Atlantic Wall.

For walkers and cyclists, the quiet country lanes and clifftop footpaths offer a glimpse of the Islands largely unseen by tourists and locals alike, while families with young children will always be able to find a safe clean sandy beach sheltered from the prevailing winds.

At low tide there are rock-pools and caves to be explored too, and talking of the tides, they are very important in this region. The range among the Islands is the largest in north west Europe, so within a mere six and a half hours the sea level can rise or fall by as much as thirty feet. Spring tides in Jersey can even reach forty feet. When the tide comes in, it really comes in! Interesting sailing for some, but also a source of continual pleasure for anyone who enjoys simply finding a comfortable spot and gazing out at a shoreline and seascape that changes minute on minute. These islands are rich in myth and legend too, but the magic is real enough, and it's all here for the taking.

Location

Despite their allegiance to the British Crown, the Islands lie very much closer to France than England. In fact, they form a relatively tight group within sight of the Normandy coast in the bay of St Michel, about 75 miles south of **Weymouth**.

Think of the Channel Islands, and Jersey, Guernsey, Herm, Alderney and Sark spring to mind immediately. There are many more, however. Some, like the **Ecrohous** and the **Paternosters**, are little more than isolated outcrops of rock; others like **Jethou** and **Brechou** are more substantial. The **Minquiers**, for example, is a vast uninhabited expanse of reef, rock, sand and shingle

Above: Cars are banned on the Isle of Sark, the last feudal state in Europe

Below: Fun on the beach of La Grande Gréve, Sark

Above: One of the attractive beaches on Herm

Below: Shoppers at Dix Neuf restaurant in St Peter Port

Above: Cliff Walkers, Torteval

Below: Statue of Victor Hugo in Candie Gardens, St Peter Port

which at low tide has a larger surface area than the entire island of Jersey. Most of the populated islands are loyal to The Queen and are considered to be a part of the British Isles, but within the archipelago there are also some French islands. People do not think of them as 'Channel Islands' but geographically speaking, they are a part of the same group. The largest is **Chausez,** which lies some 19 miles south of Jersey.

Jersey is the largest, and the most southerly, of the British Islands in the archipelago. It is roughly rectangular in shape measuring approximately nine and a half miles west to east, and five and a half miles north to south. High ground is to be found in the north of the island, low ground in the south. As a result the whole island slopes southwards towards the sun.

Guernsey is the second largest of the Islands. Unlike Jersey it slopes towards the north. It is roughly lozenge shaped and has an area of approximately 25 square miles. The population is 55,000, of whom 16,000 live in St Peter Port, the main town. In contrast with St Helier in Jersey, St Peter Port retains a nineteenth century air. Many of the streets are still cobbled and the buildings remain recognisable from Victorian prints. By sea, St Peter Port lies approximately 25 miles from St Helier.

Alderney is roughly 20 miles to the north of Guernsey and is the most northerly of the group. It can feel remote and somewhat isolated, and this is reinforced by the somewhat windswept appearance although many would argue that this is part of its charm. Despite its seeming isolation, it is in fact only a 12 minutes flight away

from Guernsey. Alderney's population of about 2,400 live within an area of about 8 sq. miles (4 miles by 2 miles).

The island has only one town, St. Anne, which is a 15 minutes walk from the airport.

Despite her diminutive size, Alderney is the only island in the group to have its own railway system and 'national' airline.

Sark is a high plateau which towers 200ft out of the sea. In total, the island is just 2 miles long. There would be two islands here were it not for 'La Coupée', a tiny isthmus a mere 10 meters wide, which joins the main area of Sark to a smaller parcel of land known as **Little Sark**. The population is about 600. Few places can be as unspoiled and beautiful. Motor vehicles are not allowed on the island. A traffic jam here would probably comprise a tractor, a bicycle and a horse drawn carriage.

You can only reach Sark by boat. There is no landing strip and planes are banned, even from flying over the Island. It has a unique system of government based on the ancient feudal system which has been long out of use elsewhere.

Herm, a mere one and a half miles in length and half mile in width, is wedge shaped. It is the home of approximately ten families – fifty-five people in total. Without roads or motor vehicles, you are free to wander where you will. It is just 15 minute's ferry ride from St Peter Port. There are no cars, no tarmac roads, and no traffic; the chances are you'll have the place to yourself all day. There are cliffs to the south of this uniquely beautiful island and a sandy common to the north. It is perhaps the closest any island can come to most peoples' idea of a desert island.

Culture

The Channel Islands' geographical proximity to France has ensured that they retain strong historical and cultural relationships with Normandy and Brittany. Victor Hugo, author of '*Les Miserables*', who spent many years living in exile in the Channel Islands described them as "Fragments of France which fell into the sea and were picked up by England".

It was this marriage between the French and English culture, which initially helped to develop a strong tourist interest in both Jersey and Guernsey. For a British public unused to foreign travel, they appeared to offer a taste of the continent within a safe and familiar English speaking environment. The weather helped of course. Jersey, for example, still claims to be the sunniest location in the British Isles.

Today, a more sophisticated public can travel much further from home, and the fear of foreign travel has largely disappeared. Despite this, the Islands still attract large numbers of visitors, mostly from the UK, but also in increasing numbers from Europe and Scandinavia. You won't find amusement arcades, funfairs or the jaded Victorian attractions typical of UK seaside resorts here, but you will find the best of food, leisure and relaxation, among Islanders who welcome visitors, take pride in their communities, and place great value upon simple words such as honesty, integrity, freedom and cleanliness.

Despite their similarities, however, each island is also unique. Victor Hugo suggested 'In Jersey you are in Normandy, in Guernsey you are in Brittany', but no matter which Island you choose, 'all is perfume, sunlight and smiles'.

Plants and animals

Long ago, the Islands were part of the European land mass. They were merely hills standing high above a low lying plain which, over the years, was submerged as the sea level gradually rose. At times, exceptionally low tides in St Ouen's bay in Jersey, still reveal the fossilised stumps of trees, remnants of a great forest which spanned the gap between the Island and the French coast. When the water rose and the high ground became cut off from the continent the easy movement of animals, insects and plants ceased. In effect, as the Islands were formed, they became both 'havens of safety' and 'prisons' – protecting and confining whatever lived there.

This process wasn't achieved overnight. The Islands were formed at different times over a long period and, as a result, species of plants and animals found on each Island can differ. Magpies, for example, are common in both Guernsey and Jersey – but rare in Alderney. In Jersey, you'll find toads but not in Guernsey. Moles are to be found in all the Islands except Herm and Guernsey. Hedgehogs thrive in all the Islands although their arrival in Sark was quite recent.

The mild climate has also played an active part in encouraging some rare plants and animals to establish themselves within the Islands. The Dartford Warbler, for example, is frequently seen nesting in the gorse banks of the

The great expanse of Côbo Bay, Guernsey

The beautiful Shell Beach on Herm. Sark is seen in the distance

Channel Islands, and green lizards are often seen clinging to old granite walls basking in the afternoon sun. Of the insects, mole crickets make a familiar summertime sound while glanville fritillary butterflies are an almost common sight among the cliffs and steep slopes of the coastline.

Holm Oaks are trees native to southern Europe, but you'll find them here too, smaller and somewhat stunted, but happy enough to take root in Island soil.

Also let us not forget the sea, the very element which gives definition and individuality to these Islands. The large tidal range hereabouts ensures that a marine biologist or anyone else with an interest in seashore life has plenty to explore and discover. The waters are warm and also remarkably polution-free. As a result, the seas and seashore

are teeming with life. Braye and Longis beaches in Alderney and Grande Havre, Vazon and Rocquaine in Guernsey, as well as the east coast of Herm, are all extremely good locations for observing marine wildlife. Here at low water you'll discover a wide variety of crabs, prawns, shrimps, sea urchins and marine plants in the rockpools.

Channel Island waters are home to shoals of mackerel, bass and mullet. In the sandy bays there are also flatfish to be caught. Further off-shore, dolphins are a regular sight.

At times, Channel Island beaches can be found swarming with birds. Gulls, gannet, and cormorants are to be found everywhere but waders, oystercatchers, ringed plover and brent geese, red-breasted merganser and grebe are also visitors. Occasionally you may be surprised to see egrett, grey heron,

Guernsey Militiaman, Castle Cornet

Le Trepied Tomb, Perelle

razorbill, puffin and even kingfisher. Vast flocks of other birds arrive in the Islands en route to and from their winter quarters.

History

It may seem strange that these Islands, a mere stone's throw from France, have such a close relationship with the UK. The reason goes back over 900 years. Before 1066, they were a part of the Duchy of Normandy. The relationship was so close that many Channel Islanders joined William and fought alongside him at the battle of Hastings.

From a Channel Islander's point of view, Duke William's defeat of King Harold at the Battle of Hastings signalled the beginning of the Channel Islands' 'colonisation' of the UK; so much for Victor Hugo's description of the Channel Islands as being 'picked up by England'. Many Islanders would argue that it was the Channel Islands which did the picking!

Ever since 1066, when Duke William of Normandy became King William I of England, (William the Conqueror), the Channel Islands have remained loyal to the English monarch. Even in 1204, when Normandy was freed of English rule, Jersey and Guernsey retained their allegiance to the crown through the sovereign's claim to the title 'Duke of Normandy'. In return for their loyalty, successive English monarchs have continued to observe the Islands' established laws, customs and liberties through Royal Charters which, among other things, have secured the independence of their judicial system and granted important privileges such as the right to tariff-free trade with England and freedom from English taxes.

The emphasis on allegiance to the monarch is an important one, for Channel Islanders draw a clear distinction between the UK monarch and the UK government. The basis of the close relationship is solely through the sovereign as the legitimate successor of the Dukes of Normandy. The Channel Islands have never been subject to UK government or administration. In effect, in most matters the two Bailiwicks of Guernsey and Jersey are self-governing.

Although many people don't like studying history, especially if there's a warm sea and a sunny beach beckoning, so much of what you see in the Islands is so directly and intimately tied in to their history, that even the briefest reading will enhance and make sense of what you see and hear.

Take up golf in Guernsey and you'll find yourself strolling past ancient dolmens on L'Ancresse Common. Go swimming and you'll be overlooked by Napoleonic fortifications or German bunkers as you take to the water. That parish church on the horizon probably contains records dating back to the time of William the Conqueror, while in St Peter Port those modern boutiques and restaurants are accommodated within buildings belonging to previous centuries. A very old church tower stands by the bus station and modern yachts and motor cruisers rest at their moorings in the shade of Castle Cornet.

In the Islands the past rubs shoulders with the present, and their story is unavoidable.

The Clameur de Haro!

As you would expect, much of the Norman feudal law at the root of island legal systems has been superseded, but it is still possible to find examples of those ancient laws in operation. The 'Clameur de Haro', for example, is an ancient Norman cry for help in which an aggrieved person kneels before witnesses and cries: "A l'aide, mon prince! On me fait tort" (Help, my prince! I am being wronged.). In some Islands this must be followed by a recitation of the Lord's Prayer in French.

The Clameur is rarely used these days, but islanders still use it now and again, usually in the sort of dispute that blows up between neighbours. It is, in effect, a do-it-yourself restraining order. It requires the alleged wrongdoer to cease his actions until a court can rule on the case.

Early history

There is evidence of prehistoric sites in dozens of locations all over the archipelago. 'Dolmen' – tombs and passage graves constructed of stone slabs – and 'standing stones' known as 'menhirs', are to be found throughout the Islands. The golf course site known as **Les Fouillages** on L'Ancresse Common in Guernsey, was discovered in 1976. Tools found there date back to around 4000 BC. The site is considered to be one of the oldest structures in all Europe.

In Jersey there are even older sites. A cave at **La Cotte de St Brelade,** for example, is said to have been occupied over 100,000 years ago.

It is uncertain whether the **Romans** ever occupied all the Islands but they certainly visited them. There is evidence of Roman activity on Alderney and a Roman warehouse has been discovered in St Peter Port, Guernsey. At the moment, marine archaeologists are working on recovering artefacts from a Roman shipwreck in the harbour.

Christianity was established in the Channel Islands by the 6th century. St Sampson was the first missionary to arrive in Guernsey. In Jersey, the hermit St Helier was martyred there in the year 555.

Marauding **Vikings** arrived in the Islands in the 9th century. The names they gave to many places in the archipelago are still used today. The Isles of Lihou and Brecqhou, for example, are derived from the old Norse word 'hou', meaning an 'islet'. The 'ey' in Jersey, Guernsey and Alderney is of Norse origin, meaning 'island'.

In later years they conquered the local population and settled in Normandy. In fact Duke William was descended from Viking stock.

Today, the **Norman** influence persists. In the Royal Court, for example, officials still bear Norman titles such as jurat (a justice of the peace), procureur (prosecutor), and greffier (clerk). Land in the Islands is also still measured in perches and vergées.

The feudal way of life has changed least of all on the island of Sark, where the Seigneur (lord) is the only person allowed to own doves and a bitch.

England's close relationship with the Islands has been a constant source of aggravation to the French. As a result, Islander's lived for centuries under almost continuous threat of invasion from France.

One of many attacks took place in 1214, led by a French pirate inappropriately known as Eustace the Monk. He specialised in setting fire to whatever he could find. By 1483 constant attacks by the French made life so bad for the Islanders that Pope Sixtus IV had to issue a Papal Bull proclaiming the Islands a neutral zone.

The Civil War

When civil war between the King and Parliament broke out in England, the Channel Islands were divided in their loyalties. Surprisingly perhaps, for an island which has traditionally owed allegiance to the crown rather than Parliament, Guernsey sided with the Parliamentary forces against the king. Islanders at the time were hurt by his recent decision to appoint an unpopular governor.

When the Parliamentarians took over, the governor and his supporters took refuge in Castle Cornet where they were besieged for more than eight years. Despite firing about 30,000 cannon balls into the Parliamentary forces in St. Peter Port, the Royalists were eventually forced to surrender in December 1651. Theirs was the last bastion in the British Isles to surrender.

Jersey took a different view of the conflict. Here the Islanders were so fanatically loyal to the crown that the young Prince of Wales took refuge in Elizabeth Castle, where he stayed for ten weeks.

Later, when Charles 1st was beheaded, his son was proclaimed King Charles II in St. Helier's Market Square. This annoyed Oliver Cromwell who retaliated by sending a force of Roundheads to the Island. They soon overpowered Jersey's defences and its militia.

The seventeenth and eighteenth centuries

The ending of the civil war brought a period of relative peace and prosperity to the Islands. Privateering and smuggling were popular activities which led to the development of more respectable occupations such as shipbuilding and barrel-making. Barrels were needed for storing and transporting wine and brandy which usually found its way to obscure and isolated English beaches at dead of night.

Peace also brought an increased interest in agriculture and an opportunity to develop legitimate forms of trade. Apple orchards produced cider for the English market, while the production of goods knitted from local wool became such a lucrative hobby that everyone took it up, fishermen and farmers as well as women and children.

The activity became so popular that the authorities were forced to ban knitting at harvest time to protect the rest of the economy. Stockings were the first big knitwear success, but later local fishermens' sweaters, known as Jerseys and Guernseys, also became good overseas earners.

German Occupation

Fort Saumarez

CAUTION

This headland is crossed by German field defences (including trenches), and some parts of the headland have recently been made unstable by coastal erosion.

Members of the public who choose to use this area do so entirely at their own risk.

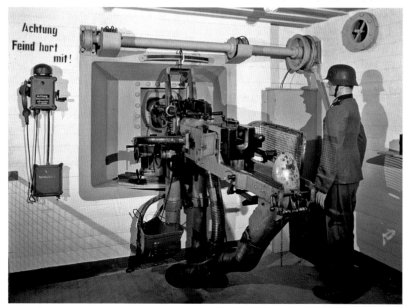

Achtung
Feind hört
mit!

Relics at the German Occupation Museum, Forest

By the late 18th century however, tension with France heightened once again and so defence became a prime concern. Round granite towers which became known as 'Martello' towers were constructed on all the coasts, and the militia was reinforced. Today, they are a prominent feature of the coastal landscape.

The French invasion came in 1781 with a force landing at La Rocque in Jersey. Initially the attack took the defenders by suprise. The Lieutenant Governor was caught in bed and surrendered immediately, but a local officer, Major Francis Peirson, refused to obey the order to lay down his arms. He engaged the French in a fierce hand to hand battle in the streets of St. Helier. Both he and the French commander, the Baron de Rullecourt, were mortally wounded, but Jersey triumphed and France never again attacked the Channel Islands.

The Victorians

The Victorians were well aware of the strategic importance of the Channel Islands to British defences, so the British government built comprehensive new fortifications throughout the Islands to counter a build-up of French forces across the water. These defences never quite equalled those of Gibraltar, but nonetheless, thanks to the Admiralty's plan to dominate the Channel, a great deal of building was done to ensure adequate protection on land and safe anchorages for the navy.

Two of the most controversial projects were the huge break-waters in St. Catherine's Bay, Jersey, and Braye Harbour in Alderney. Both breakwaters were built large enough to offer shelter to the entire fleet if necessary. Admiralty interest in the Channel Islands also led to the construction of lighthouses, as well as good roads and railways in Jersey, Alderney and Guernsey.

The introduction of regular steamship services increased the speed of communication with England, and local farmers were able to take advantage of the better climate to export their early produce. Jersey new potatoes became a familiar delicacy in England, and the fruit of Guernsey greenhouses, originally grapes, then tomatoes, also found favour in the English markets.

The Second World War

When France fell to the Germans in 1940, it became obvious to the British Government that the Channel Islands could not be adequately protected. As a result Britain proclaimed the Islands indefensible and offered no resistance to German invasion forces.

Occupation

Many Islanders, including virtually the entire population of Alderney, fled to England before thousands of Hitler's troops arrived to take up occupation. For the Nazis the occupation of the Islands was of huge significance. They were valuable for propaganda purposes and they were also viewed as a vital sector of the Atlantic Wall defences. As a result, thousands of "slave workers" were imported to build the impregnable command posts and gun emplacements. Alderney, in particular, was used in this way.

Later in the war, after the allied

invasion of Normandy, the Channel Islands remained in German hands, but the occupiers were increasingly cut off from the retreating German forces on the continent.

For Channel Islanders, this was probably the hardest time of the occupation years. They were aware of the allied victories in Europe but no relief or supplies came to them. In their isolation, both German forces and civilians in the Islands suffered extreme shortages of food, fuel and medicines. It was very late in the war before relief arrived.

Thankfully on May 9, 1945, the emaciated citizens put on their best clothes and gathered to listen to Winston Churchill broadcasting the news of all-round German capitulation. "And our dear Channel Islands are also to be freed today", he said. The vital emergency supplies which saved the Islanders from starvation and disaster arrived aboard a Red Cross ship, the *Vega*.

'**Liberation Day**' is a public holiday in the Islands.

Overnight the German occupying force became prisoners of war, and they were put to work immediately dismantling barbed wire and digging up more than 150,000 mines. Fortunately the methodical German army had posted "Achtung!" signs on the edges of minefields, so clearance was a reasonably safe and straight-forward task.

Within a month of liberation day, King George VI and Queen Elizabeth visited the Islands to encourage the recovery programme. Soon afterwards, those who had left as evacuees were allowed to return and pick up the threads of their lives. Fortunately the initial days of austerity passed swiftly thanks to rapid redevelopment.

Alderney, which had suffered greater vandalism under the occupying forces than other islands, took longer to restore.

The present day

As a visitor to the Islands, you will find much which seems familiar. Police Officers wear mainland uniforms, cars drive on the left, and public houses serve beer by the pint. Scratch the surface however, and some important differences in law will emerge. For example, the Islands are not members of the European Union, and there is no equal opportunity legislation. Indeed, many visitors are surprised, not so much by the differences between UK and Island law, but by the general lack of legislation within the Islands.

One rule which should be noted, however, is that NO CARAVANS OR MOTOR HOMES are permitted.

Local Government

The 'British' Islands are divided into two administrative groups known as **Bailiwicks**. The Bailiwick of Jersey comprises the Island of Jersey and several large uninhabited reefs and offshore Islets. The Bailiwick of Guernsey comprises the Islands of Guernsey, Herm, Sark and Alderney.

A Bailiwick is a term used to describe an area or a region governed by a bailiff. In most matters, each Bailiwick of the Channel Islands governs its own affairs. Despite their proximity and common interests, there is surprisingly little formal contact between the Bailiwicks of Jersey and Guernsey.

The Government of the Bailiwick of Guernsey is commonly called '**The States**'. It comprises the Bailiff (President of the States), twelve conseillers (elected for 6 years service), HM Procureur (Attorney General) and a Comptroller (Solicitor General), thirty-three Peoples' Deputies (equivalent to MPs) and ten Douzaine (Parish) representatives. These comprise the States of Deliberation which meets monthly. Included in their number are two representatives of the States of Alderney.

Deputies represent the ten Island parishes and are elected by the public every three years. Conseillers however, are elected by the States of Election for a six year term of office. Douzeniers are nominated by the Douzaines (Parish Councils) to serve for one year. Normally, the Lieutenant-Governor, representing the Queen, attends States meetings, but has no vote.

As the parliament of a community which is largely self-governing, the States has the power to levy its own duties in the Island, and the ability to make its own laws and run its own affairs. As a result there is no VAT charged in the Island, and the Island sets and raises its own taxes to meet the costs of all its services and amenities. By UK standards, taxes in the Channel Islands are low.

The Bailiwick has its own police force and courts of law.

Since 1830, copper or bronze coins have been specially minted for use in Guernsey. Initially they were valued in 'doubles' – eight to a penny, four to a half-penny and two to a farthing. All bore the Island arms on one side and the value on the other. Until the 1920s French as well as English money was legal tender in the Island.

Getting there

By air

There are frequent direct flights to Guernsey from a wide range of UK and European airports. Bristol, Geneva, London, Plymouth, Southampton, Belfast, Leeds / Bradford, Manchester. Flight times from Southampton and London are under an hour, for Leeds/Bradford you can expect to be in the air for about one hour and fifteen minutes.

Landing in Guernsey is a casual straightforward business. There's no stacking and little formality – except of course for the customs hall, which is only to be expected. After all, when you come to the Islands you're travelling outside the European Union.

Flights to Alderney

It is possible to fly direct to Alderney from Bournemouth with Blue Islands, and from Southampton with Aurigny, Alderney's own airline. This company also operates a number of inter-island routes and between the Islands and France. The three-engined seventeen seater Trislander's are a distinctive feature of Channel Island life. Until recently each one was painted a distinctive bright yellow. Today however, they are frequently painted in the livery of prestigious local companies. Locally, they are known as 'Joeys', because of the 'J' for joey call-sign letters painted on the wings and fuselage of the flag-

There are many boats to the outlying Islands from St Peter Port

ship plane. This aeroplane has been the subject of a large number of children's books '*Little Yellow Plane Adventures*' written by Peter Seabourne.

By sea

If you prefer travelling by sea, **Condor Ferries Ltd** operates a regular and frequent service between Poole and Guernsey. The service carries both car and foot passengers aboard high speed 'Wave-piercer' catamarans which make the crossing in about two and a half hours. There is a duty free shop on board and drinks and light meals are available on each crossing. The vessels use computerised navigation systems and the main passenger cabins are fitted with screens which display digitised charts showing the vessel's location and progress as she makes her way across the Channel. The last half hour of the journey to Guernsey is particularly interesting as she threads her way among the Islands.

On a calm day, the motion on board is more like that of an aeroplane than a traditional ferry. These are new vessels however, and their design does not permit them to be used safely in poor weather conditions so, given the nature of the English Channel, even in summer there is always a risk that the schedule of sailings will be disrupted. A traditional car ferry can be brought into service if required.

Travel between the Islands

Aurigny and Blue Islands operate regular and frequent passenger services between the Islands and also to and from France. Flights between Guernsey and Jersey for example are scheduled for every half hour. The flight time is fifteen minutes. Guernsey to Alderney takes a mere twelve minutes. These small craft fly at low altitudes, between one and two thousand feet, so the views of the Islands can be outstanding.

If you prefer sea travel, there are a number of companies which operate regular sailings between the islands. In addition, during summer months, there are additional sailings for day trippers. For Herm and Sark, the only access is by sea.

Accommodation

Accommodation in Guernsey is generally of a high standard. Hotels and guest houses in the Bailiwick of Guernsey are classified according to a 'star' system. To gain registration, they must satisfy a number of basic requirements as laid down by the Guernsey Tourist Board. A full description of system and the minimum requirements for each category is given in the FactFile.

Climate

"A climate for leisure", said Victor Hugo when he lived here. Two factors ensure that Channel Island weather is generally better than that of the UK. Firstly, the Islands are located well to the south of England, you can expect about eight hours of sunshine on an average summer day. Rainfall is moderate, about 34 inches in a year, and thankfully most of it falls during the winter period.

Secondly, they are surrounded by the warm waters of the North Atlantic drift, an ocean current which contributes

Island Languages

Queen Victoria made three visits to the Channel Islands during her reign and she was greatly pleased by the loyalty and patriotism of the people she found here. At the time, however, it is doubtful whether many of them could understand anything she said!

For centuries, ordinary Islanders communicated in the ancient languages of the Islands, forms of Norman French similar to that spoken in Normandy around 900 years ago. On formal occasions, French was the approved language. Guernsey didn't get around to making English the official language until 1921. Before that date, if William the Conqueror had returned from the dead to visit the Islands, he would probably have understood the Islanders' dialects better than anyone.

To modern French speakers however, the old Channel Island languages are Incomprehensible – like a modern UK resident trying to read an eleventh century Anglo Saxon manuscript. Today the use of these languages in everyday speech is almost extinct.

Guernsey-French, Jersey-French and Sarkees may still occasionally be heard spoken, chiefly by the elderly country people. Island children rarely use them, even though some are probably able to understand. In recent years there has been a renewal of interest in the old languages, but it is hard to imagine that their use will ever extend beyond the classroom or interest group meeting.

Alderney-French is no longer spoken at all. It was dying out before the second world war, and the mass evacuation of the Island before the German invasion in 1940, killed this language completely.

to an almost Mediterranean feel to the weather. The sea keeps the Islands relatively mild throughout the winter. On average you can expect snow to lie on the ground on only three or four mornings during the year and the number of air frosts average only 13 per year. Coastal districts can enjoy a succession of winters with neither frost nor snow.

The prevailing wind in the UK is westerly here in the Channel Island though, the winds can blow from any direction. West and west-northwest are the most frequent, although in spring northeast and east winds tend to be more prevalent.

On an island though, no matter which way the wind blows, there will always be a sheltered beach. If you find the wind blowing off the sea, take a trip to a beach across the island, it'll be sheltered there!

Although tourist authorities will tell you that sea temperatures in the Islands average 17°C in summer, this can be misleading. Such readings are often taken in relatively deep water. If you choose to do your swimming in the late afternoon when the tide has risen and covered an expanse of sand which has absorbed the heat of the sun throughout the day, the water temperature will probably be significantly higher.

2. Introduction to Guernsey

Guernsey's beaches are clearly the main attraction for a large number of visitors to the Island. If this is your annual holiday, no one will blame you for staking your claim to a patch of soft sand in a warm sunny spot with good views and spending a good deal of time there. But this isn't all that Guernsey has to offer.

Sometimes, to see the Island at its best, you need to take a more active role and turn your back to the sea for a while: after all, the ancient name for Guernsey is **'Sarnia'**, a word which meant 'Green Land' – residents are still known as 'Sarnians'. For such a small place, there's an awful lot of countryside to explore, from L'Ancresse Common

Opposite page: Fishing Boats at Les Dicqs, Vale parish Left: St. Peter Port Below: Albert Marina, St. Peter Port

in the north where the famous breed of Guernsey cattle can still be seen, to the quiet lanes and pathways which thread their way through the lush valleys in the centre and south of the island.

Geography

Essentially, Guernsey is a low plateau standing out of the sea, lower in the north, higher and somewhat hillier towards the south. The principal underlying rock is granite and, as you would expect, it has been used extensively as a building material throughout the Island. As a result, both the landscape and the architectural features are similar to those of Brittany, some 50 or so miles to the south.

Guernsey is a real working community, it has a long and fascinating history and a landscape which is remarkably varied for such a small location. The coastline is about 31 miles (50 Kilometres) – smaller than Disneyworld in Florida.

The south coast comprises a number of small sheltered coves separated by high cliffs and headlands stretching from Pleinmont to Jerbourg. This is a rugged and rocky shore but there are some delightful coves nestling hidden away behind the steep slopes and sheer cliff faces. Within the coves there are some beaches of fine white sand, and on a good day, the north coast of Jersey is clearly visible from the clifftops.

The west coast, is lower and more gentle. Large rock formations are still a feature of the shoreline, but the bays are more open and the views are generally broader.

The main feature of Guernsey's northern coast is L'Ancresse Bay, a low coast of white sand, windswept heath and big views across the beach.

The east coast is low in the north where the road hugs the shoreline often only a few meters above sea level. South of St Peter Port however, it rises sharply.

It could be tempting to drive around the island on a sunny day and visit each beach and cove, ticking off those you have visited almost like a trainspotter: 'Côbo Bay? Yes, did it yesterday!'

There are people within the Island however, who will tell you that they have visited some locations countless times throughout their lives, and still they couldn't claim to 'know them', and they certainly wouldn't want to tick them off their list for a further visit. Those massive rocks don't change, the cliffs don't move, and the beach doesn't alter colour but there are three factors which make each visit unique:– the weather, the time, and the state of tide.

Weather

In bright midday summer sunlight, most beaches present a picture-postcard image of holidaymakers enjoying the surf and warm sea. But return to a south coast cove under a lowering sky and rising southerly wind and the place takes on a very different aspect. The once clear and gentle sea becomes an angry welter of crashing foam as a succession of waves throw themselves against the rock buttresses and granite outcrops with all the speed and weight of heavy goods trains. On days such as this, these coves and headlands take on a dramatic beauty – an appropriate backdrop for the thunder of surf and the plaintive cry of storm-tossed seabirds.

Return again on a summer morning

when the Island is shrouded in mist and the place will be different again. On such days, the sea takes on an aspect of painted glass. You can hear the low throb of fishing boat engines far out to sea and yet you cannot see beyond the entrance to the cove. When the mist clings to the water and swirls among the trees on the steeply wooded valley side, tales of smugglers and pirates, secret landings and departures, all become real and believable. Sometimes it can be difficult to separate myth and legend from reality.

Time

The time of day also has a part to play. In the afternoon heat, the high angle of the sun can make distant views hazy and vague. Neighbouring islands are often little more than dark blue/green shapes viewed across a sparking sea but later, as the sun lowers in the sky and shadows lengthen in the early evening, the Islands move into sharp focus. From the old cannon mounted at the entrance to Fort Vale, for example, it is possible to look out across the water and pick out fine details of houses, fields and cliffs on Herm and Jethou. On good days, in the polished air following a shower of rain for example, even the more distant island of Sark begins to reveal some of her secrets.

Later in the evening the west coast, only four miles distant, provides some of the most spectacular sunsets.

Tides

Finally there's the tide. The waters which lap Guernsey's shore have the second largest tidal range in the Islands.

As a result, many coves and beaches change dramatically with each rise and fall. It's an ever changing picture and one which never fails to impress. 'Spring tides' occur roughly every month and at such times the tide rises even higher than usual. At the top of the tide, boats in the harbours are almost at street level. Offshore, the waves will be heavier and the currents stronger.

Spring tides

Local boatmen have a particular respect for these tides. At the top of a spring tide, rocks which are usually un-covered and easily avoided, may be lurking beneath the surface waiting to catch the unwary. Inshore, the extra weight of water travelling through the rock gullies can overpower small boat engines. In places the tide can be pulling so hard that to anchor carries the risk of having your boat dragged under by the current. Pot markers, those brightly coloured buoys which indicate places where crab, lobster or prawn pots have been laid, are often dragged under the surface. At these times fishermen have no option but to wait and return when a less fierce tide permits them to break surface once again. In the meantime, they lurk maybe a metre or so under the surface waiting to tangle with the propeller of any small boat innocently passing overhead.

A gale at the height of a spring tide, is something which every boatman fears, especially if his moorings are in an exposed location, but for visitors watching from the shore or clifftops, spring tides offers a spectacular dem-onstration of the raw power of wind

Views on the north coast

Which Bay?

These bays will be least affected by the indicated winds

North Wind
↓↓↓

Chouet
L'Erée
Fermain
Moulin Huet
Saints
Petit Bot Bay
Petit Port

North-East Wind
↙↙↙

Chouet
Portinfer
Port Soif
Grandes Rocques
Côbo
Vazon
L'Erée
Rocquaine
Petit Bôt Bay
Moulin Huet
Saints
Petit Port

South Wind
↑↑↑

L' Ancresse
Pembroke
Portinfer
Port Soif
Grandes Rocques
Côbo
Vazon
Fermain
Rocquaine
Portelet

South-West Wind
↗↗↗

L' Ancresse
Pembroke
Fermain
Petit Bot Bay
Saints
Portelet

Views on the south coast

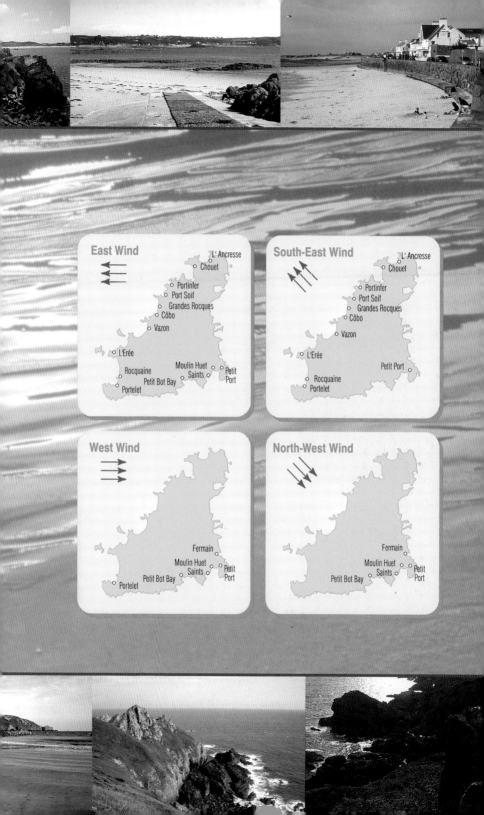

East Wind

- L' Ancresse
- Chouet
- Portinfer
- Port Soif
- Grandes Rocques
- Côbo
- Vazon
- L'Erée
- Rocquaine
- Petit Bot Bay
- Moulin Huet
- Saints
- Petit Port
- Portelet

South-East Wind

- L' Ancresse
- Chouet
- Portinfer
- Port Soif
- Grandes Rocques
- Côbo
- Vazon
- L'Erée
- Rocquaine
- Portelet
- Petit Port

West Wind

- Fermain
- Moulin Huet
- Saints
- Petit Port
- Petit Bot Bay
- Portelet

North-West Wind

- Fermain
- Moulin Huet
- Saints
- Petit Port
- Petit Bot Bay

and water. However bathers, especially children and poor swimmers, should stay well away from the water.

Spring tides reach places which a normal high tide does not attain so as the tide ebbs, the shoreline appears clean and scoured. If you like beachcombing, now is the time to see what you can find. Pots, pot markers, lengths of rope, net, mooring buoys and the occasional beach sandal, are all common finds. More rarely flags, oilskins and items of deck cargo may turn up. If you find a size seven flip-flop sandal for a right foot, let the author know, he's collected six left footed ones recently!

The intertidal zone

Just as a spring tide produces unusually high water levels, so the ensuing ebb results in an unusually low tide, exposing areas of beach, reefs and rock pools which are rarely seen. Ecologists refer to the shoreline which is exposed between high and low water as the 'intertidal zone'.

Getting around

Many visitors to Guernsey bring their own vehicle but a large number prefer to leave their car at home and take advantage of the relatively cheap car hire rates in the Island. Guernsey also has a good system of public transport, both 'scheduled services', and 'coach trips' organised to take visitors to specific locations.

Recent years have also seen developments in 'green tourism' where visitors have been encouraged to walk or make greater use of bicycles. The best advice seems to be to take advantage of a variety of options to ensure that you get the best experience available.

Bus services

Guernsey Bus and Island Coachways offer comprehensive scheduled bus services in the Island. Information about routes and schedules can be obtained from **Picquet House** by the town church in St Peter Port. These offices are a short walk from the ferry port along the Esplanade and they should be an early port of call for every visitor. The distinctive building is often mistaken for the Island Tourist Office which is, in fact, a tall granite building half way along the Esplanade between the ferry terminal and Picquet House. For some reason many visitors walk past and fail to notice it.

At Picquet House there are free maps of the Island which illustrate the scheduled bus routes and times of service. There is a flat fare of 60p for all journeys of any distance on all routes plus, there is a Wave and Save card which may save you money if you are going to make frequent use of the bus services.

Other brochures available at Picquet House give details of **Island tours**. In summer, for example Island Coachways offer a number of morning tours concentrating on different aspects of the island.

Examples include:

A **'Island at War'** tour with a stop at Fort Grey to see The Guernsey Museum "History in Action" Company's costumed presentations. The tour will then take you back on the road to see the sites that have been highlighted in the performance.

A **'Crafty Guernsey'** tour takes in the beautiful Little Chapel along with visits to see the crafts of Guernsey (candlemaker, pottery, clockmakers, and your chance to purchase a traditional Guernsey jumper). Along the way you will see the picturesque heart of Guernsey.

'Guernsey In A Day'. run weekly on a Sunday, this tour shows the best that the Island has to offer in a short time. You will see the fortifications of the island, discover the history of the occupation, and take in scenery at the Reservoir and the Little Chapel. There is a stop for lunch at the Oatlands Centre and the tour finishes at Candie Gardens, where at the height of the season, there is entertainment.

Bus routes have changed recently and may be subject to further alteration – check your destination before you board.

Car hire

Car hire is a popular option but you must remember to bring your UK license with you. In Guernsey nothing is more than twenty minutes away by car, but despite the diminutive size of the island there are many hundreds of miles of roads and lanes to explore. It's easy to become lost, but also easy to find your way to the coast in order to regain your bearings.

By UK standards, car hire rates are very reasonable and petrol, free from UK government taxes, is remarkably inexpensive. Bear in mind however, that driving in Guernsey is different!

Many roads in Guernsey are narrow lanes, with high hedges or granite walls. Few junctions are signposted. Most Is-landers know where they are and where they are going, but this isn't always the case with tourists. Be prepared to meet horses, cattle, cyclists and pedestrians at every turn – and other drivers who may be just as lost as you!

Over the years, Islanders have evolved a courteous style of driving. On a small island with narrow roads and a high level of car ownership, they have discovered that you get there quicker if you help the other driver. Frequently you'll find vehicles slowing to let you enter a main road, or drivers waving you through a right turn. It's in your best interests to adopt the same attitude – after all you're on holiday!

Maximum speed permitted anywhere in the Island is 35 mph (56 kph). There are lower speed limits in some areas. In and around the town for example the speed limit is only 25 mph (40 kph).

Drinking and driving laws are more stringent than in the UK. In Guernsey the Police have the power to make random checks.

Public parking in Guernsey is free but you will need a **'parking clock'** to indicate your time of arrival in car parks where a 'disc zone' sign is displayed. Some on-street parking places are also disc zones. You can buy parking clocks on car ferries, at the Information Bureau and the Police Station, as well as some garages and shops.

Most parking near the centre of the town is designated for short stay only (three hours or less). Long stay parking (five hours or more) is generally further away, and fills up early in the morning. The Harbour piers offer the best chance of parking in town. The largest is **North**

Water Safety

Take great care near the water – a spring tide is unforgiving. If the waves are high or confused, stay well away from the water. People have been swept off sea walls and slipways by breaking waves and they have also been lost in surf rolling onto a beach. Strong winds are not frequent in summer, but when they do occur, they don't necessarily bring rain. Conditions which whip up seas such as these often happen in bright sunlight. Don't let the sunshine lull you into a false sense of security. When the waves are high and breaking, stay away from the edge.

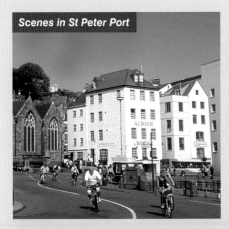

Scenes in St Peter Port

Beach where three-hour parking space can always be found.

If you're hoping to be in town for longer, or wish to leave the car while going on a day trip to the other Islands, the best advice is to take a bus or taxi, or use the **park-and-ride** service, which runs from **Footes Lane**.

Cycling

Cycling is an ideal way to explore the island. Distances between points of interest are short and the roads can be remarkably quiet out of town. In the north and centre of the Island there are few significant hills and you'll rarely need to dismount.

Exploring the south of the Island can be a little more challenging. There is a long steep and winding climb southwards out of St Peter Port and traffic can be heavy in both directions. Having gained clifftop height, visiting south-coast bays and coves can be a frustrating experience entailing rapid descents to sea level followed by steep and arduous climbs back to the main road. Fortunately, many of the roads down to the bays are shaded by overhanging trees and there are plenty of opportunities for refreshment stops. Riding north from St Peter Port is a much more pleasant experience. The road hugs the low coastline all the way to L'Ancresse Common.

As a cyclist in the Island you have several advantages over the car driver. With a bicycle you have no parking problems. In town there are lots of locations where you can simply lock your bike and leave it. There is, for example, a bike park in the centre of town in front of the Island Tourist Information Office. More importantly perhaps, on the narrow country lanes you can stop wherever you want without fear of blocking the road. This is particularly important if you are interested in bird watching or photography.

With a cycle you can enjoy the best of both worlds. Speed restrictions and relatively short distances enable you to cover ground between points of interest almost as fast as a car driver. With a cycle however, providing you exercise care and push or carry your bike when it is appropriate, you also have access to a large number of quiet pathways prohibited to motor vehicles. With a cycle, you can reach the parts which motorists can only read about. You get to meet more people too!

In preparing this book, the author chose cycling as the preferred means of transport in Guernsey, Alderney and Sark. For exploration and photography, the advantages over the car were enormous.

Walking

The Guernsey Tourist Information Service publishes a number of pamphlets containing suggested walks within the Island. There are also several other publications, including this one, which offer recommended walking routes. With 16 miles of cliff paths and countless other delightful inland circuits to follow, Guernsey must rank in the top ten of walkers' desirable locations.

Walking in Guernsey is a relaxed and pleasant activity. Some of the steeper parts of the cliff path can be a little strenuous but generally you'll find nothing here to compare with walks in say the Yorkshire Dales or the Peak District. Many of the recommended routes can be comfortably completed within a couple of hours and some are especially suited to particular times of the day. Take your time and enjoy them. Generally, published walks are well described and carefully chosen to ensure that there is plenty to see and read about en route. All you'll need are comfortable shoes and some refreshments.

If following a published walk is too much for you, try driving to one of the car parks on the south coast and then taking a short stroll along the cliff path. You don't have to walk far from the carpark to leave the majority of tourists behind. Here you'll find a quieter island with a succession of outstanding views at every turning. Coastal paths are well marked and maintained. A picnic, a good book and some sun-blocker provide all the ingredients for a perfect afternoon.

Coastal Cruises

Guernsey yachtsmen and fishermen know how beautiful their island really is. When you stand on the beach and look out across the sea, you become part of that beauty but from the deck of a small boat, weaving in close among those rocky outcrops and looking into inaccessible coves and places hidden from the clifftops, you gain a different perspective – a view of the bigger picture.

Tourist Information has details of coastal trips available. Alternatively, you could take a stroll around the harbour and read the signs and posters. Make a point of undertaking a coastal cruise. It's well worth it.

Things to do

Annual events

Certain dates in the calendar are particularly interesting for visitors:

The **St Peter Port Carnival** usually takes place at the end of July. Here you'll find impromptu performers, street entertainers and a great deal more.

Each summer Thursday afternoon you can also visit the **Old Guernsey Market** in Market Square, St Peter Port. Here you'll find traders dressed in old time Guernsey costume complete with flowing skirts, tailcoats, top hats and Guernsey bonnets.

On Market days, the square becomes a traffic free zone for the afternoon as stalls are set out and the area is sealed off. You can buy anything here from local crafts to souvenirs of your stay in Guernsey. There is music and entertainment too, so it's well worth a visit.

The first Monday in July is traditionally set aside for the **"Viaer Marchi"**, a trip back in time and an evening packed with entertainment and attractions in the beautiful setting of **Saumarez Park**. It usually begins at about 6pm and you'll find stalls, sideshows, craft exhibitions, entertainments and lots of people. This is the **National Trust of Guernsey's** major annual event so it is well worth a visit.

There are three main **agricultural shows** in Guernsey:

The first is the '**South Show**' in St Martins which is held on the first Wednesday and Thursday of August.

The second is the '**West Show**', held on the Wednesday and Thursday of the second week in August, on the

Local Produce

General store, selling Guernsey cream fudge, Market Street and the fish market in St. Peter Port

Coastal cruising

site of the old aerodrome at L'Eree, St Saviours.

Finally, the largest of the three is known as the '**North Show**'. It's also referred to as the "**The Battle Of The Flowers**". This takes place during the third week of August in Saumarez Park.

Although Guernsey is a popular location for a summertime visit, the Island also has much to offer during the 'shoulder' months of early spring and autumn. Even in winter it is an attractive quiet location, especially if you're looking to avoid the worst of the frost and snow. Some hotels and guesthouses close for the winter period but many remain open throughout the year. An affluent local population ensures that there is always a good selection of restaurants available. Many people would argue that you see Guernsey at her best outside the main tourist season. At these times, you gain a real impression of life in a small island community.

Shopping

There is **no VAT** charged on goods bought in Guernsey and so shopping can be a pleasant and profitable way to spend some time. Make a point of comparing prices with the costs of similar goods in the UK. Freight charges can occasionally erode the price differential between Guernsey's VAT free prices and those of the UK. Remember also that Guernsey is not a member of the European Union, therefore customs charges may be imposed on items which you take back to the UK with you.

Purchases which appear to offer the best value against UK prices include drinks, tobacco and luxury goods. Many visitors purchase alcohol to take home. Prices in Guernsey may be slightly higher than in duty-free shops, but the choice is wider. Locally produced wine and liqueurs are also available. Tobacco in all its forms is very cheap and there are good bargains to be found in jewellery and cosmetics. If you're bringing your car, arrive with an empty tank and leave with a full one.

The general standard of living in Guernsey is high in comparison with the UK, and therefore the shops are well stocked with a good range of quality clothing and luxury items such as electrical goods, cameras, watches and sports equipment. They aren't particularly cheap but you should be able to purchase them at lower prices than in the UK.

Most shops in Guernsey are open between 9:00 am and 5:30 pm. Some shops observe the half-day closing on Thursday afternoons, and in the country districts some still close for lunch. During the summer, many shops stay open into the evening.

Sport

If you enjoy sport, Guernsey has a great deal to offer. Its isolation from the mainland and the major UK sporting events, has made Guernsey an island of sports participants rather than spectators. So no matter what your interest, you'll find plenty of opportunity here.

A comprehensive list of sporting associations, activity centres, hire locations, and useful addresses are given in the FactFile. Details of particular events taking place in the Island are usually advertised in the '*Weekender*' a supplement contained with each Saturday's edition of the **Guernsey Evening Press**.

Particular strengths in the Island include:

Bowling

There is an indoor bowls facility at the '**Guernsey Indoor Bowls Centre**' and an excellent outdoor greens at Beau Sejour, the Corbet Field and Delancey.

Golf

The island has three excellent golf courses. The premier one is the 18 hole course at L'Ancresse. There are also courses at La Grande Mare, Vazon where a few holes double up to make it an 18 hole course and the 9 hole par-3 course at St Pierre Park Hotel.

Tennis

This is a popular game in Guernsey and there is now an impressive indoor facility at '**Longcamp Tennis Centre**'. Tuition is available for all levels.

Cycling

The tourist board have introduced six cycle tours, each colour coded. A booklet is available from the Tourist Information Centre. Cycles can be hired from several dealers on the island.

Flying

You can learn to fly with **Guernsey Aero Club** and few locations can offer such ideal surroundings in which to do it. The club also offers inexpensive 'trial flights' for those who wish to get a taste of piloting a small aircraft without making the commitment to a full course of lessons. You get to handle the controls and, even if a full pilots license isn't your ambition, a short 30 minute flight gives you a view of the Islands that will stay in your memory for ever more.

Surfing and board-sailing

While the general sporting provision in the Island is good, Guernsey's weather and close relationship with the sea gives it particular strengths in some activities. It is an ideal location for almost any type of water-based activity. The fact that it is an island also makes it a particularly good location for swimming, surfing and boardsailing. You can hire equipment in a variety of locations. Try '**Sail or Surf**' at 24 Commercial Arcade, St Peter Port, where they offer sailing, surfing, windsurfing hire and tuition every day at Pembroke Bay.

Diving

The diving and snorkelling possibilities in Guernsey are said to be among the finest in Western Europe. There is plenty of beauty and interest to be found under the waves in the bays and coves. The quality of teaching is extremely high and all levels can be catered for. With a tidal range of 10 metres plus on a spring tide and 4 metres on the smallest neap tide, Guernsey is an ideal location for drift dives. Currents can be up 9 knots in places with slack water windows of only 15 minutes.

There is some excellent wreck diving in these waters too. The **Cement Wreck** (wreck of the barge *Oost Vlaanderen*), is a good example. Her local

Sailing

Golf

Low-water Fishing

At 'low-water springs' some Guernsey residents take up low-water fishing. There are no rods or boats required, just a long stick to poke into the exposed rocky holes and crevasses where crabs, lobster and crayfish might be found; maybe a rake for collecting cockles from just under the surface of the sand; and a small trowel for knocking limpets and native oysters off rocks. Some low-water fishermen also take a small bag of salt for catching razor fish. These fish, with shells which look like old Victorian cut-throat razors, dig themselves into the sand at low water leaving only a distinctive oval hole to mark their presence. They are able to bury themselves at great speed and can usually sink through the sand faster than an adult can dig with a spade. Patience and a pinch of salt however, can achieve great things. Guernsey people place a small heap of salt over the hole and wait patiently. The dissolved salt trickling into the hole, convinces the razor-fish that the tide has returned and so it re-emerges ready to feast on whatever comes its way. A net bag or wicker basket for taking home the catch completes the collection of essential low-water fishing equipment.

Low water fishing requires a good deal of local knowledge and an understanding of the tides and the way they run across a particular beach. As a visitor, the safest way to explore the far reaches of the shore at low tide, is to follow the ebb tide down and return before it turns and begins to rise.

At certain strictly regulated times, the most serious low-water fishermen wade out into the water and run their hands over submerged rock surfaces feeling for the much prized **Ormer**, a large local shellfish which makes a delicious meal fried or stewed.

However, as far as visitors are concerned, as most don't have the facilities to cook a low water catch anyway, the best advice may be to enjoy visiting the rockpools and observe the marine environment without removing anything, and remember to replace turned over rocks before moving on. The low water shore is a fascinating but delicate place and easily damaged by the curiosity of humans.

In Guernsey you'll be frequently advised to take nothing more than photographs and leave nothing behind on the beach except your footprints.

name arises from the fact that she sank with a full load of cement on board.

For reef divers a visit to **Gold-fishers Reef** just off the east coast can be a gentle yet fascinating experience, but for the really adventurous, '**Gouliot Passage**' offers a high energy, high speed drift dive. The tide runs at up to ten knots along this narrow channel and the experience has been likened to getting into the washing machine and hitting the Turbo Spin button. It is not for the faint hearted.

For further information contact the Blue Dolphins Sub Aqua Club by email bdsac@cwgsy.net. The club offers full British Sub Aqua training and diving from boats for the more experienced.

Sailing

Several years ago, the Island community realised that looking after visiting yachtsmen makes sound commonsense. Faced with labour shortages and a lack of building space, the Islanders realised that by attracting the sailing community to their shores they were increasing the number of spending visitors without need of building or staffing additional hotels or self-catering facilities.

Few other holidaymakers would be prepared to put up with the cramped conditions most sailors experience on their boats. They also realised that such conditions tended to ensure that yachtsmen spent a good deal of their time in the shoreside pubs and restaurants. As a result, you'll find the warmest of welcomes if you arrive in the Island under your own steam, and the fact that so many people take this option, has created an entire local industry aimed at meeting the needs of sailing folk.

You can bring your own boat, charter craft here, or use the Island as a base for attending courses of tuition in all aspects of sailing. If you enjoy sailing, Guernsey has something for you.

Fishing

From shore or from a boat, there is some exciting sport to be had and, just as many of the activities mentioned above are affected by the strength and direction of the wind in relation to the shore, it is a well known fact that in stormy conditions, fish will seek the calm of a sheltered bay.

In Guernsey, the sea surrounds you, so regardless of the wind speed or direction, there is always a sheltered bay close by. You may have to cross the Island to find it, but in such a tiny place, distances are small. Likewise on most days, somewhere in the Island, you'll find a useful onshore breeze if that is what you are looking for.

Nightlife

Although in Guernsey the emphasis tends to be upon relaxation, family entertainment and outdoor and sporting activities, there is a useful nightlife to be enjoyed, especially at weekends when locals come out and let their hair down too. There is a variety of nightclubs in St Peter Port, although it has to be admitted they close much earlier than you would expect at many other European holiday centres. Many of the Island's public houses host live music events and there are two cinemas, one inside the **Beau Sejour Centre** in St Peter Port, and the other, a four screen selection, is housed at the **Mallard Hotel** near the airport.

Beau Sejour also stages live theatre during the summer months, and **St James'**, a converted church at the bottom of **La Grange** in St Peter Port, stages an annual programme of music recitals and shows. A monthly calendar of information concerning shows and recitals is available from the Information Centre and at most hotel and guesthouse receptions.

Licensing Laws

Guernsey's pubs are similar to those in the UK, and they offer a good range of cheap wholesome food but the licensing laws are different to those of the UK.

During weekdays, pubs may open their doors from 10am until 11.45pm but some close in the afternoon for a few hours.

On Sundays, opening hours are noon until 3.30pm then 6pm until 11pm, but you may only drink alcohol in the evening if you purchase a meal.

Hotels, Cafes and Restaurants are allowed one hour's extra drinking to 12.45am from Monday to Saturday though you must have eaten on the premises.

Rainy Days

Yes, they do happen, and unfortunately they can be difficult to predict. By definition a small island such as Guernsey has a 'maritime' climate and therefore you can expect a shower of rain in any season. If you are a walker or countryside lover, a brief shower should present no problem, and in any case, in Guernsey you are never far from shelter, in the form of a cafe, a public house, or maybe the sheltering wall of a church.

In longer periods of rain however, especially if you have children in the party, you may need to take advantage of some of the indoor attractions which Guernsey has to offer. Some, such as museums and art galleries have been mentioned before, and there is a summary of general attractions listed in the FactFile.

For an enjoyable rainy day with children however, check out what's on offer at **Beau Sejour Leisure Centre**. There are so many activities available there, as well as programmed events and entertainment, that you could easily spend a full day.

Eating Out

Compiling a list of good places to eat is a dangerous excercise. There are so many variables. Different people have different views about value for money and anyway, even the best of restaurants can change for the worse with just a small change of personnel. When all is said and done, as you would expect, it all boils down to a matter of taste!

Despite this, there is no doubt that Guernsey has more than its fair share of excellent cafes and restaurants. There is something here to suit every taste and pocket, from beachside cafes and kiosks with views so magnificent they almost defy description, to intimate town bistros bursting with

atmosphere and bohommie, and elegant restaurants comparable with the best you'll find anywhere in the UK or continental Europe.

A list reflecting some of the possibilities based on the author's personal taste, is given in the FactFile, but bear in mind that it is not exhaustive and quality can vary from season to season. Perhaps the best advice is to become a menu hunter. Make a point of checking out what is on offer as you travel round the island and remember those menus which seem the most interesting. Remember too that the price of a meal may be no indication of the extent to which you'll enjoy it. Some of the best fish and chips to be found anywhere in the world are on sale at '**The Bridge'** at St Sampson's harbour and they're cheap too – but an essential ingredient in their enjoyment is to sit and watch darkness fall across the harbour, the boats tugging at their moorings, and the reflections of the harbour lights flashing across the water.

If the weather is good, why not take advantage of it? Invest in a small disposable barbecue which can be bought at most supermarkets and some garages in the Island, and make a truly memorable 'al fresco' meal on the beach. Barbecued fresh local fish, grilled oysters, sausages or steak, one or two local tomatoes, a freshly baked French loaf and a glass or wine or fruit juice in some secluded spot with magnificent views..... what else do you need to create an eating occasion which you'll never forget?

Channel Islands' Shipwrecks

For centuries the rock-strewn waters of the Channel Islands were greatly feared by seafarers. High tidal ranges, strong currents, variable weather and frequent fogs all added to the uncertainty of navigating these waters, especially during periods when navigation was a less precise science than it is today.

The **English Channel** has always been one of the busiest waterways in the world and so it is hardly surprising that these coasts and reefs have provided the backdrops for some of the most harrowing tales of terror, despair and suffering ever encountered on the sea.

The first recorded shipwreck in the Channel Islands occurred in 1278 when a vessel from La Rochelle came to grief on the **Castle Rocks** in Guernsey waters. Since that time there has been an almost endless list of maritime disasters within the archipelago. The situation improved during the 1970's when the shipping lane which skirted the western shores of Guernsey was moved further out into deeper and clearer Channel waters, but the problem of navigation between the Islands still remains.

In 2002 a major disaster was averted by the Jersey rescue services when a high speed passenger catamaran, bound for Guernsey, struck a rock and had to be abandoned off Corbière Headland southwest of the Island. Fortunately, calm weather, daylight, and a well-rehearsed local disaster plan, ensured there were no deaths and only minor injuries.

Within the Bailiwick of Guernsey, around **five hundred vessels** are known to have either sunk or run aground. Such a figure should not be taken as complete, however. Undoubtedly, others went down with total loss of life without anyone being aware of the tragedy. How many ships which went missing over the years, may be resting on the bottom in Channel Island waters?

Take the wreck discovered in 1912 near **Le Hanois** in Guernsey, for example. The story goes that in August of that year fishermen reported sighting the top of a funnel and a mast covered in seaweed just under the surface of the water. Closer investigations revealed that little of the wreck remained and that the 'funnel' spotted by the fishermen, was in fact the ship's boiler. From the build up of weeds and barnacles on the wreck, experts were able to determine that the vessel had been lying on the seabed for less than a year. The mystery ship was never positively identified but one thing is clear, all those on board perished in sight of land and safety.

The most famous shipwrecks in these waters include:

The Loss of HMS Victory

In 1774, the fourth of five Royal Navy warships to carry this name, sailed homeward bound up Channel from the Mediterranean. She was a 100 gun first-rater, recognised in her day as the finest ship of her type afloat. She became separated from the rest of the fleet on the night of 5th October in one of the worst storms the Islands had experienced for many years. At 2:00am that morning the Keeper of the **Casquets Lighthouse** heard gunfire from the stricken vessel, but due to the storm they were unable to offer assistance.

The Loss of the Stella

Sometimes referred to as the '*Titanic*' of the Channel Islands, the passenger ferry '*Stella*' came to grief when she struck the **Black Rock** on the Casquets on 30th March 1899. Her master, Captain Rigg, ordered the women and children away first in the lifeboats. The rest were left on board to survive as best they could. One hundred and five lives were lost, including those of Captain Rigg and Mrs Mary Rogers, a stewardess who gave up her place in a lifeboat to help a passenger.

Other Losses

Not all shipwrecks involved massive loss of life, however. Some of the most harrowing tales involve just one or two people. Take for example the tragic tale of the '*Iris,*' a small ketch discovered aground east of **Fort Le Marchant** in Guernsey. No-one was found on board, but later a body was recovered from Fontenelle Bay and identified as the mate.

A tragic event in itself, but the tale took an even more horrific twist a month later, when the body of the boat's owner was found on the islets known as the '**Humps**,' north of Herm. The poor man had obviously managed to reach the islet from the sinking vessel and had made a rough hut there using seaweed and wreckage from the boat.

Weak and possibly injured from the disaster, he had been unable to call or signal for assistance, and he therefore died a lingering death from starvation and exposure within sight of safety.

For more information about shipwrecks in the Bailiwick, visit **Fort Grey Maritime Museum** in Guernsey.

3. The Parish of St Peter Port

The Capital – St Peter Port

No matter whether you arrive by sea or air, whether you intend to stay in Guernsey or travel on to the other islands, St Peter Port is the gateway. As the principle town of Guernsey, home of the Island's government, main port of entry, centre of the Island's finance

industry, main shopping centre and residential area for a large portion of the population, it must be high on your list of places to visit.

The town is often described as having three parts. Firstly, the old part, clustered around the town church and waterfront. Secondly, 'new town', inland from the old centre and on higher ground overlooking the harbour, and not so much 'new' as Georgian rather than mediaeval. Finally, there are relatively new housing estates which circle the perimeter.

Left: Queen Elizabeth II Marina

Old St Peter Port

It is almost certain that St Peter Port began life as a small fishing village. The coastline here didn't have the physical features necessary to provide a large natural harbour, but the shelter offered by the other islands was probably enough to enable the settlement to grow. Fishing would have encouraged the development of other activities, boatbuilding, rope and net making perhaps. Then later, traders and merchants would have been attracted to the location, transforming the settlement from a simple village to a growing seaport.

For centuries, it was an important staging post in the wine trade, used for the replenishment of stores and as a haven of safety in foul weather by ships trading between England and the Mediterranean. Later, wine was laid down here to mature before being sold on. There are still several great cellars and vaults in the town which serve as a reminder of those times.

Today, **'Town'** as Islanders call it, is one of the most attractive shopping and entertainment centres in the British Isles. The main streets, which in reality are charming narrow cobbled thoroughfares, have been largely pedestrianised. You can wander freely along winding streets and passageways which have hardly changed in hundreds of years, and everywhere, through tiny passages, or glimpsed between buildings, there are views of the harbour, the marinas, **Castle Cornet** and the sea beyond.

St Peter Port is an excellent **VAT free** shopping centre and many well known UK stores sell goods here. More than that however, the town is a place to stroll around and enjoy. The waterfront offers ever changing sights as passenger ferries and pleasure yachts come and go on the tide. There are benches all along the waterfront and you'll find plenty of other places to sit strategically placed around the town. Take your time, relax and watch the world go by.

Eating out

As well as sights and shops, you'll find a vast range of cafes and restaurants here. They offer a wide selection of food at a variety of prices. There is something here for everyone, from a burger bar, to some of the finest French style restaurants you'll find anywhere. For couscous lovers, the Clubhouse at La Collinette Hotel serves Moroccan & North African cuisine in its new 'Kashmara Restaurant'.

And yet, as if to remind you of the way in which Guernsey manages to bridge the English/ French cultural divide, you'll also find pub grub in the finest English tradition.

Obviously, fish is a speciality hereabouts and it is available on many menus. Crab, lobster, bream, sea bass and plaice are frequently offered, along with 'fruits de mer' ingredients such as oysters, mussels (moules), scallops (Coquille St Jacques) and clams.

For eating out, the range of possibilities available in St Peter Port, is greater than you would find in any English or French provincial town, and generally you'll get excellent value for money.

Places of Interest

The Town Church

As St Peter Port developed, so the original fishermens' chapel was transformed into a church which many now consider to be the finest in all the Channel Islands. Written records of the church date back to 1048. Since that time however, it has undergone several transformations. The slender, carefully constructed south transept, for example, was built in 1466 in a style which contrasts sharply with the older heavy Norman architecture of earlier parts of the building.

Outside, the massive granite masonry and the elegance of the porch are particularly noticeable. Inside, the colours of the **Royal Guernsey Militia** hang in the sanctuary, whilst the walls are covered in memorials which offer a great insight into the names and lives of the leading players in the Island's history:– characters such as the privateer Captain Nicholas Le Messurier who was killed on the high seas in 1759, and general Sir Isaac Brock who led the successful British troops at the Battle of Queenston Heights in 1812.

At times, the church served as a refuge against attack, and for many years the north aisle was 'home' to the parish fire pump. Most of the church windows are modern because the old Victorian ones had to be replaced, along with windows in a number of other buildings, following an explosion in the harbour during the German occupation of the Island. Fortunately, it is generally felt that the new windows are of a higher quality than those which they replaced.

Close by the church, almost on the quay, there is a stone pillar, known as the **'Barriere de la Ville'**. Some argue that it is one of a number of such stones which marked the sites of the gates in the town walls which Edward III ordered to be built as a defence against attacks from France in 1350. Others suggest that the stones merely indicate the original town boundaries.

The Markets

For some years the market area of town was somewhat run down and sad looking. The markets were originally constructed between the harbour and the town far enough away from the town church to placate the congregation which used to complain about the smell and the vermin from butcher businesses located close by.

The **'French Halles'** were built in 1782 but they were soon found to be too small. At the time of writing the whole market area is undergoing redevelopment.

The Harbour

No visit to St Peter Port can be complete without a tour of the harbour. The stone pier running east from the Town Church was constructed in the thirteenth century but it has undergone many changes since then. It was improved during the reign of Elizabeth I, for example. Today it is known as the **Albert Pier**. The **North Pier** was constructed during the reign of Queen Anne. Together they enclose the 'Old Harbour' which today contains the **Victoria** and **Albert Yacht Marinas**.

The range of tides experienced in the Channel Islands can often give visitors the impression that island harbours have been constructed on dry land. Many of them dry out completely at low water. The **Old Harbour** was no exception to this rule. As a result, by Victorian times additional port facilities capable of offering accommodation to shipping of much greater tonnage were needed.

Scenes in St Peter Port (below & opposite)

3. The Parish of St Peter Port

With typical Victorian energy and vision, a new pier was constructed, **Castle Pier,** stretching from the South Esplanade, by the bus station, to Castle Cornet – which had previously stood on a rocky islet, isolated from the shore. Beyond Castle Cornet, the pier continued as a massive breakwater stretching out into the sea. A granite lighthouse was constructed at the end. The whole pier, breakwater and lighthouse is a masterpiece of Victorian engineering and determination.

To the north of St Peter Port, the Victorians constructed another breakwater across the pierheads. The combined effect of the two civil engineering projects was to create a huge sheltered haven for some of the largest ships of the day.

Later, in the 1920s, the much uglier but extremely useful **St Julian's Pier** was built to provide berths for ferries, fishing vessels and cargo carriers. The Jetty attached also has a **RoRo** (Roll on Roll off) ramp for vehicles. Offices and waiting rooms for voyagers are located in flat roofed buildings on this pier. There is public access to these rooftops. They offer a panoramic overview of the port.

Today, much of the containerised freight and all sea-bourne visitors to the Island enter through St Peter Port harbour. In addition there are three yacht marinas within the complex. One marina alone, the **Queen Elizabeth II,** can accommodate up to 800 craft. The harbour is also the home port for a fleet of approximately 20 fishing vessels and numerous inter-island ferries and passenger vessels offering coastal cruising trips.

The harbour, its piers and breakwaters, are all generally accessible to the public and many of the best vantage points have seating. In the daytime it is a hive of activity with boats and ferries constantly arriving and departing. In the evening however, it is a quieter place, popular with anglers, pleasure boat crews, and visitors who enjoy strolling along the upper walks or simply gazing out to the other islands and enjoying the last of the evening sunlight.

Castle Cornet

Castle Cornet has to be seen and visited but when you do, it is important to remember that it was a military installation in almost continuous use from 1206 until the end of the Second World War. King George V1 finally presented it to the people of Guernsey in 1945 and since that time it has been a tourist attraction. Throughout the 739 years of its military use however, its architecture was in a state of almost constant change to take account of developments in weapons' technology over the years. This is no picture postcard fairytale castle, rather it is a stark reminder of the strategic importance of the site over a long period of time.

Originally, the castle was built on an isolated outcrop of rock, to protect St Peter Port and British ships trading from the south coast of England which passed between the Islands on their way to and from Bordeaux. Standing isolated in the bay at the top of the tide it must have been a formidable sight, especially when the keep was still intact prior to 1672; in that year lightening struck the structure which was being used as a gunpowder store, and the resulting explosion both destroyed the tower and killed the wife and mother of the Governor of Guernsey.

Today however, views of the castle are less impressive due to the pier and breakwater which, in the mind's eye, now firmly anchor the castle to the land.

Whilst views of the castle may not have improved over the years, there is still plenty for visitors to see both in the castle and from its walls and ramparts. The range of military architecture is huge. You'll find everything here from medieval walls to German bunkers. There is an entrance fee, but once inside you can wander around freely or take advantage of a guided tour.

The entrance is through a doorway and under a portcullis in the bastion. As you enter, you'll see above you a battery of cannon, pointing towards the harbour. Traditionally they were used to fire the salute to visiting ships of state. A cannon is still fired from the Royal Battery inside the castle at noon each day in the months between April and October. It is very loud. Even if you are expecting it, the noise can come as a surprise.

In summer, flowers are used to soften the stark concrete and granite of the ramparts. From here the views of the town, the harbour and the other Islands can be magnificent.

The castle also houses **five museums** which chart its history from its initial building to the present day. There are permanent exhibits including collections of uniforms and arms, pictures and relics of the occupation. Refreshments are available in the 'refectory' which was formerly the married quarters of the garrison.

Victor Hugo's house

The continuing success of the West End musical 'Les Miserables', adapted from Victor Hugo's famous novel, has aroused a good deal of interest in this strange Frenchman who adopted Guernsey during the French Revolution and made **Hauteville House** his own during his eighteen years of exile.

Having upset Louis Napoleon and the future Napoleon III in his writings, he fled France to live in Jersey on 5th August 1852 but his stay in that island was brief. Three years later, in October 1855, he was expelled for supporting the editor of a local journal who published a letter offensive to the crown.

Unable to remain in Jersey and fearful of returning to France, he promptly established himself in Guernsey, and it was at Hauteville House that he created his most famous works.

During his stay at Hauteville, he transformed the house into one of the most extraordinary examples of interior design imaginable. Strategically placed mirrors meant that from his top floor studio, he could see anyone coming up the stairs long before they arrived. His enthusiasm for DIY had no limit. The panelled walls and much of the furniture were constructed from old Guernsey chests and boxes. To describe the house as 'bizarre' would be an understatement.

His study was on the top floor of the house. It had a large window from which he enjoyed a panoramic view across the town to the harbour and beyond to the islands of Herm and Sark. It was from here, in 1862, that he penned 'Les Miserables' – perhaps his best remembered work today.

Castle Cornet and the lighthouse

Victor Hugo's former home, Hautville House

HAVTEVILLE - HOVSE
MAISON D'EXIL DE VICTOR HVGO
1856 - 1870
A ÉTÉ OFFERTE À LA VILLE DE PARIS
PAR
JEANNE HVGO
ET LES
ENFANTS DE GEORGES HVGO
EN MCMXXVII

Victoria Marina

For many people, however, 'Les Travailleurs de la Mer' (The Toilers of the Sea), a later though less well-known work, is still considered to be his masterpiece. The story of this book is set in Guernsey. He completed it in 1865 and dedicated it to the people of this island:

'I dedicate this book to the rock of hospitality and liberty inhabited by the noble little nation of the sea. To the Island of Guernsey, severe yet kind. My present asylum, perhaps my tomb' Victor Hugo, Hauteville House, Guernsey 1865.

It is a classic tale of 'man against the elements' and throughout the book his love of the Channel Islands, and Guernsey in particular, shines through. If you're looking for some holiday reading, there is no better book to read while in the Island. It is published in paperback by Guernsey Press and is available in most bookshops in the Island. Armed with a good map and an enquiring mind, you will find that many of the locations mentioned in 'The Toilers' are still there, waiting to be rediscovered.

The best place to begin such a voyage is Hauteville House. Today it is the property of the City of Paris and is maintained as it was during the time when Victor Hugo owned and lived in it. It is open to the public daily for guided tours. As you would expect, Hautville House attracts a large number of French tourists. There is a limit to the number of visitors which can be admitted into the house on each tour so you may have to wait a while to gain access. Parking close by is very restricted, the best advice is to park in the harbour and walk up the hill.

Guernsey Museum and Art Gallery

Across town in **Candie Gardens**, you'll find a statue of Victor Hugo standing on a granite rock gazing out towards France. Close by there is the Guernsey Museum and Art Gallery. Displays tell the story of Guernsey, beginning with the Island's geology, climate and natural history, and moving on through the Neolithic and Iron Age periods to the present day. The art gallery changes its displays regularly. The building also houses a shop, a small theatre and a cafe. It is also the home of **La Societe Guernesiaise**, a very active and important 'learned' society committed to researching many aspects of Guernsey culture and heritage. The Museum earned the 'New Museum Of The Year' award in 1979.

1 & 2 Walking tours of the capital

You can enjoy a stroll around the harbour or the streets of St Peter Port at any time, but if you prefer more 'structure and purpose' to your meanderings, try one of the following walks:-

The High Street, The Royal Court, and War Memorial

It is almost impossible to explore St Peter Port by car or bus, there are far too many pedestrian areas and one-way streets. So begin by taking a bus to the Bus Station at **Picquet House** or by leaving your car nearby at the harbour. Take a look at the **Town Church** if you haven't visited it already and then wander up the **High Street.** Until about 60 years ago, all the old town of St Peter Port was paved in this way.

Unfortunately in places, more modern materials have been used when repair work has been needed. Still though, you'll find plenty of the ancient paving remaining in parts of the High Street, **Le Pollet**, **Contrée Mansell,** and in other lanes and alleys along the way.

As you go, try to ignore the shop fronts and the contents of their windows. Look instead at the architecture. Until about 150 years ago, road conditions in the Island were such that the wealthy who owned large residences in the country, also had 'town houses' in order to avoid the need for regular travel along roads and tracks which, at best, were always uncomfortable and occasionally impassable. Hiding behind these modern shop windows, are the old town residences of the wealthy. Some of today's shops are operating from very fine old buildings.

Much of medieval St Peter Port disappeared long ago as the population, wealthy through trade and privateering, tore down the ancient buildings in favour of newer and more comfortable constructions. Half way along the High Street however, you'll find the entrance

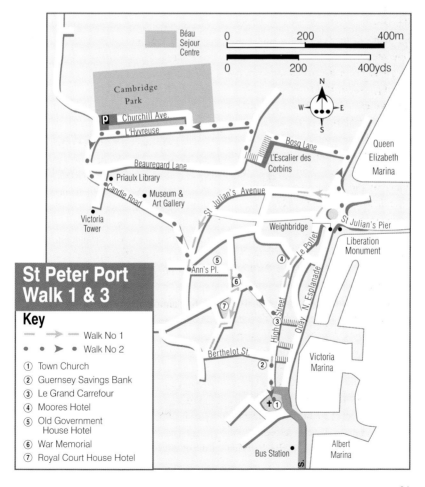

St Peter Port Walk 1 & 3

Key

- — ⇒ — Walk No 1
- • • ➤ • Walk No 2
- ① Town Church
- ② Guernsey Savings Bank
- ③ Le Grand Carrefour
- ④ Moores Hotel
- ⑤ Old Government House Hotel
- ⑥ War Memorial
- ⑦ Royal Court House Hotel

May 9th Obelisk

By St Julian's Weighbridge you'll find a single needle-like column comprising fifty pieces of local polished granite, representing the fifty years since the liberation from German occupation. It was erected and designed by local artist Eric Snell. David Le Conte, a former NASA scientist, undertook the necessary calculations to ensure that on 9th of May each year, the obelisk casts its shadow onto different plaques mounted along a low wall close by. Each plaque commemorates a particular event, and the shadow falls on each plaque at the time the event took place!

to **Guernsey Savings Bank**, which still maintains its medieval character. Close by, Berthelot Street also maintains some medieval characteristics. We'll explore that later.

Further along the High Street you'll find two alleyways which provide quick access to the Esplanade and quays. Locally they are known as '**venelles**'. There is a third venelle known as **North Pier Steps** at the top of the High Street.

The place where the High Street meets Le Pollet, Smith Street and the North Pier Steps, is known as '**Le Grand Carrefour**' (the great crossroads – well, great by Guernsey standards at least!). Le Pollet is known as '**The Pollet**' by Guernsey folk, and 'Pollet Street' by visitors. This is a narrow ancient cobbled street which leads northwards towards to the shore. Cannon balls have been discovered in the walls and buildings here, fired by the Royalist forces when they held Castle Cornet during the civil war. The small shops along the street generally complement the architecture. Although they are modern, they do not detract from the overall impression of an old busy thoroughfare in a small trading port.

Moore's Hotel at the end of Le Pollet, was once the town residence of the de Saumarez family, a very powerful Guernsey dynasty. Across the street, there is a shop which used to be the residence of Sir Edgar MacCulloch, who founded the Societe Guernesiaise in 1882.

Moving on, a stroll along **Lower Pollet** takes you past more shops and restaurants to **La Tourgand**, a spot where once stood a medieval tower guarding the northern approach to the town.

Albert Marina

Today, it is the location of **St Julian's Weighbridge**, an attractive stone building with a watchtower. It's a busy place for traffic travelling to or from the harbour or using the Esplanade to travel across town. Despite this, it's worth spending a little time just watching the world go by. Ticket offices for boat trips to Herm and Sark are located here and further along the road into the harbour.

Returning to our walk, you can leave much of the noise and the traffic behind by heading inland along **St Julian's Avenue**. Here, some way along the Avenue, you'll find a garden containing an unusual statue of a soldier standing guard over a wounded comrade. It was erected in remembrance of Islanders who fell in the South African war.

Turn left along **Ann's Place** at the top of the Avenue and you will pass the Old Government House Hotel which, as its name suggests, used to be Government House. The War Memorial is close by at the end of Ann's Place, and the Royal Court House in Rue du Manor is a short walk from here.

The Island **War Memorial** is particularly important. As a self-governing community, Guernsey's population is not obliged to undertake military service in wartime. To its credit however, the Guernsey States waived the right of exemption from military service in both world wars. Casualties were particularly heavy among Islander's during the final battles of the First World War.

The Royal Court House was built in 1799. It houses the States of Deliberation (the Island Parliament), the Royal Court Chamber, and the Greffe (record room) where important public documents are kept. It is an unlikely but very interesting place to visit. The Island's government meets there on two days each month, and in addition, there are Magistrates, Juvenile, Petty Debts, Civil or Royal Court hearings, sitting daily.

At the rear of the Court House is the former Prison. A few yards higher up the hill there is the unusual disused church of **St James the Less**, which is now a concert hall.

Passing in front of the Royal Court takes you to the **Odd-fellows Hall** and a parish water pump. A short climb up **Lefebvre Street** gives you a glimpse of the former prison at the rear of the Court House. From here turn left into **New Street** and climb to the highest point of this walk, the junction with **Berthelot Street**. At this point you are close by the **Salvation Army Citadel** which can be visited by climbing onto **Clifton Street** and walking a short way along it. Alternatively drink in the atmosphere of times past by ambling back down to the town centre along medieval Berthelot Street. It's a simple descent back to **Market Street** and the place of your departure.

2. The south of Town and Hauteville

An alternative walk from the Town Church begins with a stroll along **Fountain Street**, past the market halls to **Le Petit Carrefour** (the small Crossroads) from where you can set off along **Le Bordage**, which remains an interesting old street despite several modern developments. A steady climb from here leads you to **Trinity Square** and the **Holy Trinity Church** which was constructed in 1789. From the outside the church has no great appeal, but the interior has been recently restored.

Passing in front of the church, follow the main road for a few more yards before turning into **Contrée Mansell**. This is an area of antique shops and interesting old pubs. Continue on along Contrée Mansell into **Mansell Street** and you'll gain an insight into how St Peter Port probably looked a hundred years ago. On the way, look out for a flight of steps on your right called the **Ruette Marie Gibault**. Opposite, there are more steps known as **Burnt Lane**. In St Peter Port all tiny lanes such as these are worth exploring.

Follow the steps up Burnt Lane and

walk past the old school entrances on your right. Notice the 'Boys' and 'Girls' entrances inscribed 'Garcons' and 'Filles'. Further along the lane there is the church of **Notre Dame de Rosarie** built in 1829 and reconstructed in 1962. Its roof is shaped like an upturned boat.

Past Notre Dame, take the left hand fork to descend to the street and from here you can stroll up **Le Vauvert** (left fork up the hill; no entry to traffic) to the Plough Inn. Just opposite you'll find a narrow steep lane known as the **'Cat's Ladder'** leading to **St Joseph's Church** which was built in 1851. The spire was added in 1885. From here

St Peter Port Walk 2

Key
1. Town Church
2. Market Halls
3. Holy Trinity Church
4. Notre Dame de Rosarie
5. Plough Inn
6. Hauteville House

Cruise along Guernsey's South coast

Herm Seaways operates a cruise along the south coast on most summer afternoons, leaving from St Peter Port harbour. The launch threads her way among the moored yachts, passes through the pierhead, and turns southwards. From the deck, you gain an excellent view of Castle Cornet and the breakwater with the lighthouse at the end. She then crosses **Havelet Bay**, with its anchored boats and tidal swimming pools along the shore. From here she sails on across Soldiers' Bay and round Fermain Point before entering **Fermain Bay**, one of the most beautiful places in the Island.

Across Fermain Bay, you'll discover the tiny fishing harbour of **Bec Du Nez** with the Pine Forest behind it. Rounding St Martin's point, the launch then skims past Telegraph Bay.

From here on the cliffs, which had been gently wooded, become grander and more rugged, and the launch hugs the coast much more closely. The views on this part of the journey are spectacular especially as she passes **The Pea Stacks**. No view of them from the shore can really do them justice.

La Gouffre

At **Petit Port** look out for the huge **Cannon Rock** towering above the beach. Here you'll see some of the steepest cliffs in Guernsey. Across **Moulin Huet Bay**, you'll discover **Bon Port**, an inlet with cliffs so sheer that it cannot be reached from the land.

Further on, **Saints Bay** is less dramatic, but it has a delightful fishing harbour and Martello tower. The cliffs become more impressive again as the launch heads for **Icart Point**. This is the highest point of the island and so, as you would expect, the granite cliffs are massive. A short way beyond is **La Bette Bay** and the dark and mysterious looking **Dog's Cave**. Imagine that place in the face of a howling southerly gale!

Close by, you'll see **La Jaonnet Bay**, an excellent place to explore, although access is steep in places. Past the cliffs of **Mont Hubert**, the launch brings you to **Petit Bôt Bay**, a beautiful beach at the end of a long steep road which winds its way down a narrow wooded valley to the shore. The fine sand here is overlooked by a Martello tower and, close by, the **St Clair Battery**, which stands guard over the bay from a low headland. If your stay in the Island is short, this bay takes priority above all others on the south coast. It must be visited, especially if you have children with you. Beyond Petit Bôt there is **Portelet Bay**, a sandy and secluded spot but difficult to reach.

In Guernsey waters, the tides control everything and so, at this point, you may find the launch turning around to make the trip back to St Peter Port. If the tide is fair however, you may continue to **Le Gouffre** and the dramatic cliffs at Les Sommeilleuses, finally turning for home in the shelter of **La Point de La Moye**.

you can follow the road around and retrace your steps to Mansell Street and on into **Mill Street**, descending later to the Market Square via the '**French Halles'** in Market Street.

If you still feel like walking, return to the Town Church, and set off climbing southwards along **Cornet Street**. The Headquarters of the National Trust of Guernsey are located halfway up the hill. Here you'll find the **Trust's Information Centre and Victorian Sweetshop**. Make a point of visiting – it's well worth the effort.

A derelict church, dedicated to **St Barnabas** built in 1874 stands, at the Summit of Cornet Street. This was the site of the Town's southern defences. From here, you could take a broad flight of steps descending to **Le Bordage** and **Cliff Street** and on towards the **South Esplanade.** It is much better however, to ignore this route and concentrate on climbing towards **Hauteville**, one of the town's most attractive areas.

The road from St Barnabas' Church begins with old and modest buildings on either side but as the way steepens, the buildings become grander. Today, many of them are private hotels. Despite this, they have lost nothing of their beauty. Here on the left, you'll find **Hauteville House**, the home of Victor Hugo.

At the top of the road, turn left into Havelet and follow the narrow, winding road back down to the sea. As you descend, the road gradually widens, offering glimpses of the waterfront between the buildings.

3. Along the Esplanade and into the parks

(see map on page 61)

You can begin this walk anywhere along the Esplanade but in view of the fact that we have started the previous walks from the Bus Station, it might be more interesting to begin this one from somewhere else   the **Weighbridge** for example.

Head northwards past the Royal Hotel which used to be one of those rather grand town houses owned by the rich and powerful, and just beyond, turn left into **Bosq Lane.** When **Les Canichers** crosses your way, take a look down this old and rather strange

Victoria Tower

looking street which begins in St Julian's Avenue and lead out towards the northern suburbs. Then set off up the steps known as **L'Escalier des Corbins**. There are some stretches of level pathway between the flights of steps so the climb is more gentle that it would first appear. At the end of L'Escalier you'll arrive in **Les Côtils**. Here there is a belvedere with seats and a viewfinder which makes the most of the clear-weather view from here.

Castle Carey, not a castle but an imposing nineteenth century mansion, is a short distance further up L'Cotils. The Duke of Cambridge visited the Island about a century ago and stayed here.

Just beyond, you'll find **Cambridge Park**, originally called 'New Ground', but renamed in honour of the Duke's visit. Enter the park and walk westward along **Winston Churchill Avenue**. It was here that the last duel in Guernsey was fought.

Across the park, **Beau Sejour Centre** offers a wide range of entertainment and sporting opportunities to locals and visitors alike. In wet weather, it can be a particularly attractive destination for tourists.

Turn left at the end of Winston Churchill Avenue and head towards the 100ft (30.5m) **Victoria Tower** which was built to commemorate the Queen's visit in 1846. You can climb it if you like. The key is obtainable from the Museum and Art Gallery, Candie Gardens from Spring 2008. As you would expect, the views from the top are magnificent. Beneath the tower in the well-kept gardens, there are two German guns, relics of World War I. At the start of the occupation, they were buried, well out of sight of the occupying forces. They remained hidden away until after the liberation.

From here, retrace you steps to **Candie Road** and take a look at the **Priaulx Library**. It is open to the public and contains an excellent collection of local books and genealogical records dating back to 1563. Close by, the **Candie Gardens** are well worth visiting. In the upper gardens, you'll find statues of Queen Victoria and Victor Hugo. The lower gardens are well sheltered and particularly interesting for their range of colourful trees and shrubs.

The **Museum and Art Gallery** is well worth a visit. From the bottom of Candie Gardens, St Julian's Avenue leads you directly back to the Weighbridge. Alternatively you can cross the road to Ann's Place and the Old Government House Hotel, and then stroll down Smith Street into the High Street, and along to the Town Church and the Esplanade.

From here the way back to the Weighbridge takes you along the waterfront, the temporary home to visiting pleasure boats of every description. The waterfront buildings are made up of a mixture of styles, and the largest are not always the most interesting. One of the most attractive belongs to **Marquand's Ship Chandlery**. An Alladin's Cave of nautical gear, you could almost expect to smell tallow and tar as you enter.

4. Castle Cornet and La Vallette

One other walk is worthwhile. Aim to do this when you have plenty of time. It takes you to Castle Cornet and so you may as well take in a visit to the castle at the same time. There is a rather steep climb at one point.

Begin at the Bus Station and walk southwards along the road past the **Albert Marina** and then turn left along the southern arm of the harbour. Before Castle Cornet, you'll arrive at the **Guernsey Yacht Club**. In front there is an expanse of water which, in Victorian times, was the model boat lake. It seems to have lost some of its attraction these days, perhaps because it has been destroyed twice. The first time was during the First World War, when the site was used as a French seaplane base. During the Second World War it was destroyed again when the

German occupying forces fortified the area. A German bunker still remains close-by. There is a refreshment kiosk here. Alternatively, refreshments are available within the castle should you decide to visit.

From here, a walk along the pier to the **Old Lighthouse** can be pleasant in settled weather. In the evening, the view of the Islands can be delightful. On a rising tide there'll be lots of anglers here. In the morning however, look back towards the town. In the sunlight, the windows shine like jewels and St Peter Port shows off her origins – old houses huddled together, clinging to the seafront and the hill beyond. Look out for the towers of St Barnabas', Elizabeth

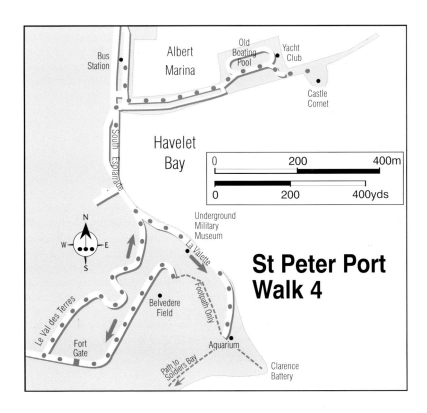

69

Getting Married in Guernsey

(rules applying to a British citizen)

In order to marry by civil ceremony or in a non Church of England church, a licence must be obtained from the **Registrar General.** For all marriages, you must ensure that two witnesses, both of whom must be over the age of 18 years, attend your ceremony and sign the marriage register.

Civil and Non Church of England Marriages

These may take place only by way of a certificate, a licence or a special licence of the Registrar General. **Civil marriages** can take place at the Office of the Registrar General, at **The Greffe** in the Royal Court House or at **St. James Assembly Hall.** Unless authorised by a special licence, your marriage can only be solemnised between the hours of 8.00am and 3.00pm.

Only one of you is required to **give notice** of your marriage in person, to the Registrar General at the Greffe, Royal Court House, St. Peter Port. However, it would be helpful if both of you could attend, so the questions about both of you can be answered without the need to make another appointment.

You **cannot give formal notice more than three months prior** to the date of your marriage, but you should contact the Office of the Registrar General at The Greffe as soon as possible after you have decided to be married, so you can be advised on the form of notice most appropriate to your circumstances, and (in the case of a marriage to be performed by a Registrar) so that a provisional date and time can be reserved. One of you must then attend at The Greffe to give formal notice of your marriage so that your reservation can be confirmed.

Marriage by Licence

Marriage by licence is usually most convenient for non-residents. To be married by licence, the person who gave notice must have resided in Guernsey for at least **seven days immediately preceding** the day on which notice of marriage is given. After seven clear days from the day your notice was entered in the notice book, a licence authorising your marriage to be solemnised will be issued.

Upon issue of either a certificate or licence, your marriage may be solemnised at the Office of the Registrar General (Monday to Friday between 9am-12.30pm and 2-2.30pm, Saturday 10am-11.30am), at St. James Assembly Hall (Monday to Friday, 9am-12.30pm and 2-2.30pm) or in a place of worship licensed for marriages by the Royal Court. Please note, the Office of the General Registrar at the Greffe is open on alternate Saturday mornings.

If you wish to get married after 3pm (but no later than 4.30pm), you need to apply for a special licence (see next paragraph).

Church of England Marriages

If you wish to get married in a church of the Church of England in Guernsey, **no reference to the Registrar General** is needed. All arrangements are made by the minister of the church in which your ceremony is to take place.

After your marriage has taken place, the minister will notify the Registrar General of your marriage.

Documentation

In order to give notice of your marriage, you must provide copies of your full **birth certificates** and sign a declaration that there is **no legal impediment** to your proposed marriage. You will also need to show documentary proof of your freedom to marry, if either of you have been previously married. If you are a **widow**, you must produce your **marriage certificate** as well as your late husband's **death certificate.** If you are a widower, you need only produce your late wife's death certificate. If you have been divorced, you must produce a court-sealed or certified copy of your **decree absolute** or final decree.

In addition, for non Guernsey residents, you will need to provide a **certificate of no impediment** confirming that you are free to marry your partner. Application for such a certificate should be made to the **Registrar** in the district where you ordinarily reside. If any of your documents are in a language other than English, they must be accompanied by officially certified translations in English.

Check with the Registrar General that your documents are satisfactory before you make your journey to the Island.

Further information

For further information and advice about getting married in Guernsey, telephone the Office of the Registrar General on +44 (0)1481-725277.

Alternatively, write to the Office of the Registrar General at The Greffe, Royal Court House, St. Peter Port, Guernsey, GY1 2PB, Channel Islands.

College, St James' and Victoria Tower.

Returning along the pier, turn left at the red granite slaughter house and walk along the road skirting **Havelet Bay**. At the brewery, follow the coast road southwards. This is **La Vallette**. It's a quiet place as most of the south-going traffic remains on the main road which climbs and winds out of St Peter Port at this point. Between the climbing road and the coast road, there are wooded slopes, beautiful gardens and steep cliffs rising to **Fort George**. Not a fort these days, it is actually a small housing estate. The main barrier gate of the old fort still stands, however, the only substantial reminder of former times.

Down by the road at La Vallette, there are swimming pools filled and refreshed twice a day by the incoming tide, lots of seats and benches and one or two places where you can obtain refreshments while taking in the views. La Vallette is close to town, and yet it remains a remarkably quiet, green and tranquil spot.

Opposite the first of the three swimming pools, you'll find **La Vallette Underground Military Museum**, a collection of memorabilia from the occupation, housed in a tunnel which formerly held the fuel tanks for German U-boats.

The **Aquarium** close-by is also located in a tunnel. It has a collection of both local and tropical fish. A path

Sailing by the Marks

Navigation in Channel Island waters is a very tricky business. How do Guernsey skippers manage their crafts with such ease under these cliffs, in such strong currents, among rocks which are as sharp as shark's teeth? Obviously, they are navigating according to knowledge and wisdom which has been passed down through countless generations of Guernsey folk.

The technique used is known as '**sailing by the marks**'. Basically, a skipper has a library of important views stored in his memory. When, for example, this particular rock appears in front of the gable end of that house on the headland, then he knows exactly where he is. He follows that course keeping the two objects in line until a rock off his starboard bow lines up with a window in a Martello tower. At this location, he knows that he must change course to avoid a particular hazard ahead of him. A Guernsey Skipper knows hundreds, possibly thousands, of 'marks'. He knows what the current will be doing at any point on the coast at any given state of tide and he knows how much water he has under his keel in each location.

Often, you'll notice that 'back markers' are used. The skipper keeps his boat on track and out of danger by keeping landmarks and seamarks in line behind him. If you see him keeping his eye on where he's been, rather than where he's going, don't be alarmed! It's OK, he's using 'back markers'.

climbing above the Aquarium leads to **Clarence Battery**, an excellent viewpoint, and then on to **Soldier's Bay** where the military used to bathe.

If you're energetic enough, the path then continues up the hill to **Belvedere Field** where, in past times, military parades took place. There are some vast panoramic views, ever changing according to the weather, the season and the time of day. Walk through **Fort Gate** and then turn right on to **Le Val des Terres**, a road which was opened in 1935 by the Prince of Wales, later to become King Edward VIII. The road winds down and emerges at the foot of Havelet Bay. It's a short walk back to the Bus Station from here.

Rural St Peter Port

St Peter Port may be the urban capital of Guernsey but it is also a parish just like nine other Guernsey parishes. Like the others, it too has a rural aspect. Inland on the outskirts of town, **Montville Gardens** are well worth a visit. The gardens are peaceful and secluded, and they offer excellent views of the town below.

An interesting excursion into the lanes and byways can be made by taking a bus to **Les Baissières.** Ask to be put off at **Friquet Junction** and from there walk northwards to the next junction and then turn right at **Rue Cohu** where there is a fine double arch to be seen. Turn right along the busy **Landes du Marche** until you reach the crossroads, then turn right again along Longue Rue.

Leave **Longue Rue** in favour of **Abreuveurs Road** and at the fork, take the right hand into **Les Canus Road.** There is a bus stop here where Canus Road joins the **Route des Capelles** but if you aren't ready to return to town just yet, you could ignore the bus stop and follow the Route des Capelles southwards. This road becomes known as **Marette Road,** and later **La Route du Coutanchez.** Follow it to the end and you'll arrive in **Rue de la Pitronnerie.** Carry straight on at the crossroads and via **Le Bouet** you'll arrive on the coast a ten minute walk from St Peter Port.

Although the coast road is busy, and the buildings along the sea front are occasionally indifferent, the walk back to town can be very pleasant, with extensive views of the islands all the way along the road.

4 Northern Parishes

St Sampson's

An electric tram car used regularly to make the trip from St Peter Port harbour to the harbour of St Samson three miles to the north. Those days are gone however, so today, if you're visiting St Sampson from St Peter Port, you have the choice of riding by car, bus or bicycle, or walking there along the coast road. There is much to be said for making the journey on foot, one way at least. It will take you no more than an hour and for part of the journey, you'll have pleasant grass

verges and plenty of places to sit down and admire the view.

For cyclists, it's an ideal and easy way to leave St Peter Port. The road is low and level for the entire journey and you can choose a route which hugs the coast all the way. In contrast, the southern exit from St Peter Port is characterised by a long, steep and winding climb.

Belle Grève Bay

Not only are there outstanding views of Herm, Jethou and Sark from this eastern shore, but as you cross Belle Grève Bay, which stands between the two harbours, your view is usually enhanced by bird life, white sails straining in the breeze, the constant coming and going of inter-island ferries, and the occasional arrival and departure of larger passenger ferries and cargo ships. Fishing boats are everywhere, and occasionally too, you'll see the tall masts of a French or British sail-training vessel anchored in the 'roads' outside St Peter Port, or maybe a cruise liner decanting her passengers, eager for an afternoon's tax-free shopping in St Peter Port.

The marina at **Salerie Corner** marks

the southern end of Belle Grève Bay. It is a popular 'all year round' swimming spot and a large crowd congregates here each New Year for the annual 'dip'. There is access to the beach via slipways at Long-store, Red Lion and Bulwer Avenue.

Belle Grève Bay is a popular beach for tourists and locals. For children there is an interesting mix of sand and rocky areas to explore, and fishing from the beach is quite good. There used to be two Martello towers along this bay. One, at Houge a la Perre, was destroyed in 1905 to clear the path for tram lines. The other, opposite the Red Lion, was demolished in 1959 for more obscure reasons.

Le Chateau des Marais

En-route along the bay, if you have the opportunity, it is worth making a short quarter-mile detour inland along **Le Grand Bouet** and **Ivy Castle Lane** to visit Le Chateau des Marais, (the castle in the marshes), locally known as the **Ivy Castle**. The castle, which is thought to date from the twelfth century, stands on a mound above a housing estate built on what used to be a low-lying marshy area. Although disused for a very long time, the walls of the castle have been recently restored, and the main gate and the eighteenth-century powder magazine are both in good order and worth seeing. As you would expect, the Germans fortified it during the occupation and one of their buildings still survives.

Back on the coast road, there is a choice after Belle Grève Bay. Either you can travel to St Sampson's harbour inland along **Grandes Maisons Road**

and **New Road** or, if you wish to stay with the coast, you can take a right turn at **Richmond Corner** and travel along **Bulwer Avenue**.

St Sampson Town

The coastal route takes you past oil tanks and warehouses which no-one would describe as pretty but, if you love the sea, you'll agree that they have a certain charm about them. They are just as important to the life of the Island as the farms, fields and cattle, so if you want to know Guernsey and understand more than the superficial, this area shouldn't be avoided.

From Richmond Corner, the 'inland' route to the harbour also has plenty to hold your interest. **Le Grande Maison**, for example, stands in **Les Grandes Maison Road**. It used to be the country house of the Le Marchant family whose town residence is now the Royal Hotel.

Delancey Park

Brock Road, off New Road, is also worth taking a look at. Here you'll find a former inn, the Anchor and Hope, with a fine archway and just a little further along there are the old '**Maisons de Bas** and **de Haut** (the lower and upper houses). At the upper extremity of Brock Road close to the Roman Catholic Church of '**Our Lady, Star of the Sea'**, there is Delancey Park, where there are some excellent seaward views to be enjoyed while the children make use of the playground.

On the slope close by the playground

is the base of an **obelisk** which used to commemorate **Admiral Lord James de Saumarez**, a remarkable Guern-seyman and contemporary of Nelson (1757 - 1836). James was present at almost every important naval engage-ment during this tempestuous era. He was made a Lieutenant during the War of American Independence. He was present at a fight with the Dutch near the Dogger Bank in 1781, and he served under Sir Richard Kempenfelt helping to capture a French convoy.

In 1782 he was one of the captains at Sir George Rodney's great victory over the French in the West Indies and, at the beginning of the war with Republican France in 1793, he was knighted for his capture of a 36-gun French frigate *'The Reunion'* off Cherbourg. In 1795 he was placed in command of the 74-gun *'Orion'* when Lord Bridport defeated the French near Brest.

In 1797 he received the King's gold medal for his part in Sir John Jervis's victory off Cape St Vincent, and at the Battle of the Nile, he was Nelson's second in command. In 1808 he was made Commander in Chief of a force operating in the Baltic sea during the ice-free summer months and for five successive seasons his forces supported Sweden against the French, ensuring the safety of vessels trading in the area. Each winter his fleet was brought home to re-fit and then used to support Lord Wellington's armies fighting the French in Spain. If ever the French needed an excuse to invade Guernsey, James de Saumarez provided it.

Sadly, the obelisk commemorating his achievements was destroyed by the Germans when they fortified the area during the occupation. Plaques recall-ing his achievements however, are now preserved at **Castle Cornet.**

On the northern slope of the hill overlooking the tennis courts there is a ruined **dolmen** which was discovered in 1919, and on the hill's eastern slope there is a bowling green. There are more German bunkers here and an earlier gun battery.

St Sampson's harbour

History

Until 1806, the northern part of Guernsey was isolated from the rest of the Island by a channel known as **Le Braye du Valle** which ran from St Sampson's on the east coast, to Grande Havre in the west. The channel was drained on the orders of Lieutenant-General Sir John Doyle, the Lieutenant Governor of the Island, who feared that the relative isolation of the north-ern parish might make it an attractive landing place for French invaders and difficult to defend.

The harbour was constructed after the draining and reclamation of the Braye at a time when the export of granite stone from quarries in the north of the Island was a thriving industry. Before the harbour was built, the in-dustry relied upon loading stone onto vessels which were grounded at low tide in creeks off the Braye, a difficult task involving transporting large and heavy rocks along cart tracks to various loca-tions on the beach at low water. After the building of St Sampson's harbour, vessels still took the ground at low water but at least the use of cranes from

sheltered and well constructed quays helped with the loading and unloading of vessels.

St Sampson's harbour is the 'industrial' port of the Island. You'll find ships here discharging oil, coal, timber, cement and all the other bulk items which are essential to the life of a small isolated community. Although the harbour lacks the prettiness of St Peter Port, it is full of character and atmosphere. Think of it as a monument to nineteenth-century energy and values.

The building of the harbour encouraged many enterprises. The nineteenth century saw the development of grape production in the Island, grown mainly in large greenhouses, originally heated by coal and wood brought in by the granite ships. St Peter Port, at the time, would not have been capable of handling such large vessels and so the industry located itself by St Sampson's to keep down overland transportation costs. Later, the emphasis shifted to tomato production in oil-heated greenhouses.

The 1960's saw a vast increase in size of the industry as modernisation took place and larger areas of glass were created, not just here but all over the Island. In the late 1970's however, the industry went into decline partly due to competition, and partly because of the oil crisis which raised fuel prices and made local tomatoes unacceptably expensive.

Since then there has been a shift to the growing of other crops such as flowers, mainly freesias, roses and carnations. Kiwi's and peppers have also been tried although more success has been had with cherry tomatoes and potted plants. Today, many of the great glasshouses have been demolished.

South Quay

Arriving at the southern side of the harbour, the first impression is one of solid civil-engineering. At low tide, when you stroll down the slipway onto the drying harbour floor, the outstanding quality of nineteenth century masonry work in the pier walls cannot be denied. Dressed stone such as this is rarely produced these days. In particular, pay attention to the finely-built southern break-water and to the **Martello tower** and other fortifications overlooking the entrance on **Mount Crevelt.**

The innermost portion of the harbour is protected by a jetty known as the **Crocq.** It is an ideal location for mooring small boats during the worst of the winter weather. It has a clock tower and obelisk marked with the names of the committee members who arranged for its building in 1872.

St Sampson's church

Behind the warehouses on the southern side of the harbour, you'll find St Sampson's church, built on the top of a beach which was reclaimed from the sea a long time ago. It marks the spot where St Sampson landed and brought Christianity to Guernsey in AD 550. The church is thought to be the oldest in the Island. It also shares the distinction of being one of only two churches in the Channel Islands which have 'Saddle-back' steeples. The other is **St Brelades** in Jersey. The solitary bell in the tower was cast in 1759.

Although much of the church building is quite recent, it is thought that some of its wall incorporate parts of a much older structure. It has a rugged style unlike any other church in Guernsey, although it has similarities with St Brelades and a church at Mont St Michel in Normandy. Inside, there is an interesting and obvious contrast between the ancient masonry of its walls, and the Victorian glass in its windows. In the north aisle, there is the chapel of **St Magloire**, a kinsman of St Sampson. It has an Easter Sepulchre where, prior to the reformation, the Host was exposed at Easter-Tide.

In the **Chancel** there is a memorial tablet recalling Lieutenant Thomas Falla who was killed in 1799 by a wound from a solid 26lb cannon ball which struck him and lodged itself between the two bones of one of his thighs. Apparently, the ball was not discovered by the surgeons until after Falla's death. The inscription in French suggests that the entire army was 'surprised' by the discovery! In the graveyard there is a memorial commemorating the loss of the SS *Channel Queen* in 1898.

The Reservoir

By the side of the graveyard is a reservoir, which in former times had been a quarry until the crushing plant was destroyed by the Germans during the occupation. One company did begin working again after the war, but in 1969 there was a landslide in which graves from St Sampson's fell into the quarry. This marked the end of the quarrying operation.

After the accident, the area was landscaped afresh and a stone cross was erected to mark the location of a mass grave where the remains of the bodies which fell into the quarry were re-buried.

The Bridge

Travelling along the road around the harbour you'll come to the 'Bridge' at the extreme western end of the harbour. Don't spend too much time looking for it though – you'll never find it! Today there is a parade of shops on the spot where the bridge used to stand, spanning the Braye to unite the northern part of the Island with the south. The shops themselves are known as '**The Bridge**'.

In the centre of the Bridge there is a boundary stone marking the border between the parishes of St Sampson and the Vale. The numerous shops at the Bridge offer a wide selection of goods.

North Quay

Just past the Bridge on the northern side of the harbour there are **shipyards**, a reminder that shipbuilding was a major industry in the Island during the nineteenth century. At one time there were yards here, on the shore at Belle Grève

Bay, and also in St Peter Port. Between the years 1820 and 1900 nearly 200 vessels were built hereabouts. Some were small fishing vessels but others were quite substantial ships including **Tea-Clippers**.

The end of sail however, signalled the end of these yards. They were not equipped for steamship construction, and only one steam vessel, *The Commerce,* was built here. For several years after the introduction of steam, the yards continued to work, picking up business in ship repair rather than building. Gradually however, one by one, they ceased trading. The last one, which continued working to within living memory, belonged to Peter Ogier. It was located on the south side of the harbour by the coal store.

Today, the quays on the north side of the harbour are interesting places to visit. Stroll around and you'll find boats of every description, and in every state of repair. Occasionally you may find one of the fast **catamarans** which ply between Guernsey and St Malo beached here. The power station, with its strange steel chimney reminiscent of a 'soviet style' of engineering, towers over the shipyard and dominates the entire north side of St Sampson's harbour.

Rural St Sampson's

Inland from St Sampson's Harbour there is the modern village of **L'Islet** and close-by on **Route Carre,** there is the **Guernsey Freesia Centre** where you can see two acres of Freesias under glass at different stages of growth.

Oatlands Craft Centre is also close-by on **Braye Road.** It has been built on the site of an old brickworks and is the only building in Guernsey to have a thatched roof. It is open from 10:00am to 5:00 pm each day and visitors are able to watch glass-blowing, silversmithing, and pottery-making taking place. There are Shire horses and a small animal farm, as well as a 'decorate it yourself' workshop. As you would expect, the on-site craft shop sells much of the produce, as well as crafted goods from elsewhere.

The craft firms which operate from here are some of the most successful Guernsey export companies. Glass bottles for the French perfume industry are produced here, and paperweights, trophies and engraved tankards are exported world-wide.

Just a little way south at **Les Petites Capelles**, **Guernsey Candles** offer free entry to their candle-making workshop where you can see a vast range of candles in all stages of production.

Vale Parish

As you stroll northwards along the line of shops at **The Bridge**, you pass from the parish of St Sampson into 'The Vale'.

The power station and shipyard are both in Vale, as is the massive stone chimney which marks the place where John Mowlem & Co had their offices and granite crushing mills. They were an English company which quit their Guernsey operation in 1929. The mill continued operation under other owners for several years afterwards however.

Places of Interest

Vale Castle

A short distance further northwards stands Vale Castle, located by the coast road atop a steep hill overlooking St Sampson, Bordeaux harbour, and the northern approaches to the Island. A recent archaeological dig revealed that this mediaeval castle was built on the site of an iron-age fort. Probably, even before then, it had been used as place of refuge. The walls and arched gateway date from the fifteenth century, and inside there are explanatory signs which point out the eighteenth century barracks, used as housing between the wars. The Germans added to the fortifications during the occupation.

The walk to the top of the castle hill is steep but short and well worth the effort because the views from here are the best in the whole of northern Guernsey. From here, all the inhabited Channel Islands can be seen. To the north, Alderney and the lighthouse on the notorious **Casquets Rock** are clearly visible, while to the south on a clear day, the north coast of Jersey forms part of the southern horizon. At the base of the castle there is a pleasant sandy beach, an ideal spot for watching the fishing boats come and go from Bordeaux harbour, just half a mile to the north.

Bordeaux

Bordeaux Harbour was the inlet chosen by Victor Hugo as the setting for his novel *The Toilers of the Sea*. Crammed with small fishing vessels, it is probably the most beautiful of Guernsey's natural harbours. There are two jetties on the south side of the harbour which make particularly good swimming platforms at high tide. A footpath runs right around the shore. There are seats and refreshments here too. The houses around the harbour are generally very attractive and substantial. **Maison Bordeaux** at the head of the inlet is thought to be of great antiquity. The stone house of **Les Rocques Barrées** (the Barred Rocks) is more modern but equally attractive.

Vale Windmill stands above the waterfront houses. It is a granite structure which was increased in height and taken for military use by the Germans during the occupation. Their handiwork was not subtle and their handiwork cannot be mistaken.

Les Hommets

By following the road around Bordeaux Harbour, you come close to **Hommet**, a 'high tide islet' at the northern end of the Bordeaux inlet. There is a car park here. Hommet is easily reached at the right state of tide, and offers good views of **Les Houmets**, a group of three islets well known for the richness of their vegetation, their wild flowers, and the sense of solitude they instil in their visitors.

The closest is **Houmet Benest.** You can stroll out to this islet most of the time because it is surrounded by the sea for only a brief period at the top of the tide. It is covered in dense vegetation but once there you'll find a German gun position and, if you are lucky, you may stumble upon an earlier gun battery, hidden by vegetation. It was built during Napoleonic times to

View from Vale Castle looking out towards Herm

Vale Castle

Russian Guests

There is little written history about Vale Castle although it did gain some notoriety in 1799 when Russian troops were quartered there. At the time, they were Britain's allies, fighting alongside English troops in the Netherlands. It was illegal to billet foreign troops in England however, so for rest and recuperation, they were sent to Guernsey and housed in a variety of locations in the Island, including Vale Castle. They were not liked by the local population.

Not so far from here, the farmer of **Les Duveaux** farm discovered one of the Russian soldiers who had been quartered at Delancey stealing his apples. He challenged him but the Russian ignored him and continued taking the apples. The Guernsey farmer was so enraged that he shot the Russian dead, and then fled the Island, making a new life for himself in the USA. He was the founder of **Guernsey County** in **Ohio**. The family cradle from Les Duveaux farm eventually also made the Atlantic crossing and can now be seen in **Cambridge**, Ohio.

It is said that when the Russians eventually sailed from Guernsey, the guns of Castle Cornet were trained on their vessel, to encourage them to give no thought to returning!

Martello Towers

Throughout the Channel Islands you'll hear and see references to 'Martello' towers. Put simply, they are nineteenth century granite built towers dotted along island coasts as focal points for the defence of the community when under threat of attack and occupation.

But how did they get their name? And, how can I tell whether the tower I am looking at is a 'Martello' tower and not some other kind of defence built before or after?

Well, first of all, when you consider that these islands were once part of the Duchy of Normandy, and are so much closer to France than England, it is hardly surprising that they needed to be defended in some way. There was no way, after all, that the French would have been happy to sit back and allow the English to keep the Islands all those years since 1066 without attempting to regain control, especially after King John's loss of Normandy in 1204.

Fortification, therefore, was the way in which the Islanders preserved their independence from the French. Over the years a variety of architectural designs were used, and towards the end of the eighteenth century 'towers' became a favoured defensive structure, because they made it possible to hold a position using muskets rather than cannon: there was a shortage of cannon on the English side, when France became America's ally in the War of American Independence in 1776.

The real advantage of coastal defence towers was not taken seriously however, until 1794, when thirty eight French troops armed with only one six-pounder and two eighteen-pounder guns in a round tower at **Mortella Point** in Corsica, managed to withstand and defy the might of the British Navy for two days of heavy fighting. In fact, the French only surrendered when the parapet caught fire.

When Britain was faced with the possibility of French attacks on the British Isles, the lessons learned at Mortella were not lost on the planners and strategists. The answer was to build towers similar to that encountered at Mortella, along the south east coast of England, the coast most vulnerable to attack from France. Later, additional towers where built along the east coast.

In the Channel Islands, there was already a history of tower building and strictly speaking, some towers in the Channel Islands should not be called Martello towers, because they were built before the battle at Mortella Point had taken place.

Only three towers in Guernsey can, in truth, be called 'Martello Towers'. These are the towers at **Fort Houmet**, **Fort Saumarez** and **Fort Grey**.

They are distinctive because of their shape, like that of an upturned flowerpot. A further fifteen towers which dotted the Guernsey coastline, some now destroyed, are pre-Martello constructions.

protect Bordeaux harbour from attack from the north.

Houmet Paradis, is the central islet in the group. Its name is derived from a nearby estate bearing the same name. Houmet Paradis features in *Toilers of the Sea,* although Victor Hugo describes it as a promontory rather than an islet. This is the largest of the group. Here you'll find traces of fields and evidence of quarrying, as well as the remains of German gun emplacements.

Just a little way further north, lies **Hommetol** which at low water stands amid a landscape best described as a wilderness of rocks. It is smaller and wilder than the other islets in the group. Although it is relatively easy to walk to Hommetol from the beach at low tide, there is a great sense of isolation here. It is a place where gulls' cries seem even more plaintive than usual, where the sea can be constantly heard, and where the wind seems to moan even on the calmest of days. Perhaps these are the reasons why it is visited less frequently than its neighbours.

The Dehus Dolmen

Just a little way inland from Houmet Paradis, on Rue du Dehus, off the junction of La Route de Bordeaux and **La Rochelle Road,** there is a Neolithic passage grave known as the Dehus Dolmen.

It was originally excavated during the nineteenth century and the pots and other artefacts which were discovered here can be seen in the **Guernsey Museum.** The Dolmen has four side chambers and is roofed over with a mound of turf, a piece of reconstruction work which was carried out during the

1930s. The structure is 30ft long, 11 ft wide at its widest point and about 6ft high. There is a car park on the opposite side of the road.

During the summer months the structure is open to the public during daylight hours and there is no entrance charge. The interior is illuminated, there is a light switch by the wooden door at the entrance, but it is a good idea to take a torch with you. A torch helps you see into the nooks and crannies, and it can be especially useful if the main light fails. Pay particular attention to the stones at the end of the chamber. On one of them are the roughly carved hands and face of a bearded figure said to be holding a bow and arrow. The lighting in the Dolmen has been specially arranged to cast shadows which accentuate this carving.

Beaucette

Beaucette Yacht Marina is just a little way north of here. You can get there by continuing northwards along Rue des Déhus until you reach a right turn into **Miellette Lane.** This brings you to the shore close by the islet of Hommetol. From here, Beaucette is a short scramble along the beach. Alternatively, by road you pass **Paradis House,** and further on, an even older dwelling now used as a store. St Magloire is said to have built a chapel hereabouts. The yacht marina lies just a few hundred yards beyond.

This was Guernsey's first marina. Originally it had been a quarry, but when it ceased working, there was only a very thin barrier of rock separating it from the sea. Breaching the barrier created an almost 'instant' marina. Today,

Beaucette provides a comprehensive range of services for sailing people. There is also a modern restaurant overlooking the marina which caters for both yachting people and visitors.

L'Ancresse Common

Compared with other parishes, Vale is reasonably flat and low lying. As such, it is an ideal location for a great deal of outdoor activities. Head for L'Ancresse Common at this northern tip of the island at any time when the weather is reasonable, and you'll be surprised by the amount of sport and outdoor activities taking place on and around this windswept expanse of low lying coastal heath and common land. On any Sunday morning for example, you may find shooting and archery, cycle racing, marathon or triathlon events, golf, wind-surfing and horse riding. It is also a spot which is much valued by fishing people and bird watchers, by families looking for soft sand and safe sea bathing, and by anyone interested in military or historical architecture.

Among all this activity there will also be walkers simply enjoying a stroll in some of the most beautiful scenery on the Island. L'Ancresse Common is a special place which must not be missed. Choose a day when it's not too windy, and spend it at L'Ancresse – you won't be disappointed.

There is plenty of discrete car parking, and the place is well served by public transport. Buses to L'Ancresse include 6, 6A, 7 and 7A. Those running to **Pembroke**, set you down almost on the beach. Buses which serve the eastern end stop a short distance away.

Fort Doyle

L'Ancresse begins at Fort Doyle at the extreme north eastern tip of the island. This fort was one of the many coastal defences built by Sir John Doyle in the eighteenth century. As you would expect, it was given a new lease of life during the German occupation, and so today, much of what you see owes its origins to a somewhat restricted period of time in the middle years of the twentieth century.

Platte Fougère Lighthouse

Just offshore there is the Platte Fougère Lighthouse which was built in 1909. It is an unmanned station supplied with power by a cable from Fort Doyle. The structure is best described as functional rather than pretty but it has probably saved the lives of a large number of seafarers. More than one ship sank on this reef before the lighthouse was built.

Fort le Marchant

A short way to the west, across the somewhat rocky shores of **Fontenelle Bay,** Fort Le Marchant stands at the end of Guernsey's most northerly promontory. It is well worth a visit. From here you can look westwards across the whole expanse of the common towards **Fort Pembroke** at the western extreme of **L'Ancresse Bay**.

L'Ancresse Bay

Today, L'Ancresse Bay is a popular beach. The anti-tank wall provides shelter from the wind and a smooth surface on which to sunbathe. The water is shallow, clear and warm, especially on an afternoon tide which has

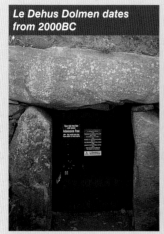

Le Dehus Dolmen dates from 2000BC

Rousse Tower

War-time Defences

Whenever Guernsey has been threatened with invasion, the occupiers have understood the attraction of L'Ancresse Bay to an invader. Its relative isolation, the gentle shoreline, the absence of cliffs, and the space to muster troops and equipment make it an ideal location for an invasion. It was the

need to be able to move troops here swiftly which led to the draining of the Braye du Valle in 1806, and it was also for this reason that the forts and **Martello towers** were built in such close proximity.

Standing by **Fort Le Marchant** you can look towards **Fort Pembroke** along the line of Martello towers flanking the shore and understand how they would have subjected invading troops to withering fire as they disembarked and struggled up the beach through the surf.

Neither was the importance of holding this beach lost on the Germans. Having strengthened the defences of both forts, they destroyed one of the Martello towers but made full use of the others. Then they built an anti-tank wall along the top of the beach. Today the Martello towers are designated ancient monuments but, strictly speaking, they are not 'Martello' towers at all. They were constructed before the term came into use.

The Millennium Monument stands on the highest point of the golf course, Vale

La Varde is now part of the golf course landscape

run across sand warmed by the heat of the morning sunshine. At low water there is a pleasant expanse of sand for children to play on. At both ends of the beach there are refreshments available. Most people seem to prefer the western end of the beach so, if you want a more secluded spot, head east!

For those who are looking for an even greater degree of seclusion, try walking around the **Le Chouet Headland** and following the path to **Baie de la Jaonneuse**. You can take this path further if you like. From here it leads westward towards a quarry containing a large German tower which, in a previous existence had stood on the summit. Beyond the quarry, the path passes another Martello tower before returning to the common.

La Varde Dolmen

Other things to see at L'Ancresse include La Varde Dolmen, standing on a site which had been heavily fortified by the Germans. Fortunately they didn't interfere with this structure. From here, on a clear day you can see Alderney and the Casquets.

Les Fouillages

Les Fouillages stand by a green on the golf links below La Varde. This Megolithic Burial Chamber was discovered in 1977 and excavated over a four year period 1978/81. The Director of the 'dig', Dr Ian Kinnes, Assistant Keeper in the Department of Prehistoric and Romano-British Antiquities at the British Museum, believes the site to be 7,000 years old and of great importance – probably unique in Western Europe.

This part of Guernsey is rich in ancient remains. Close by, for example, there is the tomb of **La Platte Mare** but even this pales into insignificance in comparison with Les Fouillages.

The west coast

Grande Havre lies to the west of L'Ancresse Common and marks the western end of the Braye du Valle, the problematic channel which isolated Vale from the rest of Guernsey until it was drained in 1806.

Today Grande Havre is 'home' to a small fishing fleet which moors in **Les Amarreurs** Bay. The clean waters also support a small oyster fishery.

For swimming, the best place is **Rousse Pier** on the southern side of the bay. As with L'Ancresse beach, the water is warmer when it rises over sand and rocks which have basked in warm sunlight during the day. After a sunny afternoon, an early evening high tide can develop 'Mediterranean' water temperatures. At low tide, it can be a beach-comber's paradise. For sandy beaches, try anywhere between Le Chouet and Les Amarreurs.

Travelling southwards from Grand Harve to **Les Grandes Rocques,** the road begins at the Rousse headland where the restored eighteenth-century loopholed tower must not be missed. **Rousse** is a pleasant spot where you can wander among the fishing craft and admire views across Grande Havre.

St Sampson's coast

From here the road turns southwards. It is a pleasant journey, along a coast with sand, rocks and sparkling sea views at every turn. With the sea in the west, this is the coast of spectacular sunsets but the ride can be confusing to anyone keeping a close eye on Parish boundaries. A glance at a parish map will show that although Vale parish crosses the water and claims land to the south of Grande Havre, St Sampson holds a tract of land along this coast too. Parish boundaries are probably of only passing interest to the majority of visitors however, and so, for the sake of convenience, this stretch of coast is mentioned here. No offence to St Sampsonites is intended!

Inland there isn't much of interest to see but on the coast **Port Grat** is a pleasant sandy spot which for some reason seems to attract few visitors. **Pecqueries Bay** by contrast is quite rocky. At low tide, neighbouring **Portinfer Bay** is an ideal location for surfing. Finally, just on the northern side of Les Grandes Rocques, **Port Soif** is a delightful, almost circular bay contain-ing two tiny islets offering the chance of exciting exploring for families with children. A coastal path threads its way among the dunes, linking all three bays. There is car parking on the headlands.

Vale Church

Finally, no visit to Vale can be complete without seeing Vale Church which has stood on this spot for perhaps a thousand years. The stonework in the **chancel** is the finest example of Norman masonry to be found in any church in the island and the sanctuary arch is also well worth seeing. Outside in the church yard, there is an early monument, probably a menhir, which was unearthed in 1949. At some stage, it has had a cross carved on it, probably to 'christianise' it. For centuries there was a priory here but this was demolished. It stood where the rectory is now located.

Stay Safe

Visit '**Les Houmets**' at low water but don't swim or wade hereabouts because the sea is very dangerous. When the tide comes in, the currents are extremely strong between the islets and the coast. To visit in safety you must know the time and you must take account of the state of the tide. Don't rely on a passer-by to tell you what the tide is doing – he may know less than you.

Make a point of checking the tide tables and planning your trip carefully. Most tables give times of high and low water according to Greenwich Mean Time (GMT). If you are visiting in summertime (BST), you'll need to adjust your calculations to take account of this. If for any reason you are marooned on an islet, stay there until the tide ebbs. You may be bored but you will be perfectly safe.

On no account should you attempt to wade or swim back to shore

---

Castel

With an area of 2,525 acres, Castel is Guernsey's largest parish. It is sometimes known as the 'Upper Parish', a reference to the fact that it stands on

Produce is often seen for sale along the roadside

relatively high ground overlooking the lower-lying parishes to the north. It takes its name from the belief that an ancient castle, Le Chateau du Grand Sarrasin, belonging to a Danish pirate Geoffroi, once stood on the site of the parish church.

Castel
Parish Church

Visit the church, you'll see why it is so easy to accept such an idea. The site, on the Route de l'Eglise close to the junction with La Rue de la Presbytère, commands a wide view, ideal for both observation and defence. Certainly, as with other church locations, there is

evidence to suggest that it had been in use long before a church was built there.

In 1878, for example, a menhir in the form of a female statue was unearthed from the floor of the chancel. Today it stands by the west porch, 2 metres tall. It has been mutilated, possibly by the people who buried it, but despite this it has still been possible to estimate its origins as tenth century BC.

The stones at the feet of the menhir used to be located at the northern end of the churchyard and it was here, until a century ago, that the officials of La Cour du Fief Lihou used to assemble, a reminder of Guernsey's more recent feudal past.

Close-by, there is a red granite trough which may have found its way to the church from nearby **Les Fontaines Farm**. The carvings of the sun and moon on the trough are thought to be sixteenth century.

From the outside, the parish church doesn't look very different from other churches in the Island. Inside however, there is a great deal to see. The **bell tower** is supported by four columns, one of which has had a piece taken out (a 'squint') so that the congregation could see the high altar when it was situated in the north chancel.

Similarly, there is a low side-window on the south side of the **nave**, so that lepers, who would not have been allowed to join the congregation inside the church, could attend mass from within the churchyard.

The **wall paintings** within the church date back to the thirteenth century. One represents the last supper, another is of a hunting scene and a

third may well represent St Thomas a Becket.

The church is located on the edge of its parish. Legend has it that the original intention was to build it at **Les Eturs**, a more central location, but the **fairies** who inhabited Les Eturs demolished the work of the masons each evening so that eventually, in despair, the builders gave up their efforts and selected another location.

Talbot Valley

Not so far from the Church, Talbot valley is considered to be one of the most beautiful pieces of countryside to be found anywhere in Guernsey. From the church, set off in a westerly direction past **Fair Field,** noticeable because of the stone obelisk standing in the middle of the field, erected in 1860 as a reminder of the cattle shows and fairs which used to take place here. Almost opposite, you will find the Ruette des Touillet. Follow this lane, turning left and then right into La Rue du Ponchez. A further turn to the left takes you downhill via the Rue du Torval and into Route des Talbots and Talbot Valley. Alternatively, you can take a bus from St Peter Port (Route 3).

The Mills

The valley extends from **Les Poidevins** to the **Kings Mills**, and there is plenty to see:– rich countryside, old buildings and a delightful mill stream, all set against a backdrop of low hills. **Les Niaux** is the one surviving mill which would have been fed by the stream in past times. It has been restored and is well worth seeing. It is not far from here. Simply walk up the valley road for a few yards, turn right, and cross the stream to reach the waterwheel.

Returning to the valley road, it is a short descent to a cottage around which runs the **Ron Short Walk**, a path leading past the cottage garden, through a copse and re-emerging on the valley road further down the hill. The path is owned by the National Trust for Guernsey who maintain it in memory of Ron, one of its most active supporters.

Further down, the road turns to the left and rises a little by an unusual old stone gateway leading to **Le Groignet** estate where vines are still cultivated. Soon, you'll arrive at the left hand turning off which there is **Le Moulin de Haut** (the upper mill). This area used to be known as **Les Grandes Moulins** because of the number of mills to be found here. The Kings Mills, close-by, are described in the chapter on the parish of St Saviour. Today the water treatment plant is built on the site of **Le Moulin de Bas** (the lower mill).

From the water treatment works, walk up **Rue de la Porte** between the estate on the left and the site of **St Anne's Chapel** on the right, and at the crossroads, you can take **La Houguette Road** down to Vazon Bay at the southern extreme of the parish.

The Coast

If you're coming from Grande Havre in the north you enter Castel parish at Les Grandes Rocques.

Les Grandes Rocques

As the name suggests, this headland is remarkable for its granite rocks, boulders and usual fortifications. Refreshments are to be found close-by. Grandes Rocques are easily reached by bus (3A), and there is ample car parking, but for walkers, there is an alternative means of arriving here. Take a bus (2, 3A) from St Peter Port to **Saumerez Park,** and having visited the grounds and the **Folk Museum,** it is a pleasant walk to Les Grandes Rocques from here.

Many Guernsey people remember Les Grandes Rocques for two spectacular shipwrecks, both of which have occurred since the war. The first, in 1973, was the wrecking of the giant ore carrier the *Elwood Mead*, the second disaster was when the oil rig, *Orion*, met a similar fate. Fortunately both vessels were salvaged.

It is a pleasant walk southwards from here along Côbo Bay to Vazon Bay. The path hugs the shoreline all the way and if you're using public transport, there's no need to return. Buses (7, 7A) all stop here.

Saline Bay

Southwards from Les Grandes Rocques, the sands of Saline Bay are very popular and from here **Côbo Bay** is only a short stroll away. This is a favourite spot for both residents and tourists. There is excellent swimming and sunbathing here, as well as plenty of rocks and pools to climb and explore and, as you'd expect, there is good surfing and board-sailing when the wind and tide are favourable. A boardsailing school and a small fishing fleet operate from here too, taking advantage of the shelter offered by the off-lying red granite reefs.

Much of the shoreline has been built

Above: Castel church *Below: Côbo Bay*

Below: Côbo Bay and Saline Bay

upon and developed since the war, but sail west from Côbo and the first place you'll come to is the American Continent. As a result, the views along the beach and to seaward are as unchanged and as impressive as ever. About halfway around the bay, there is a small shopping centre with a supermarket, newsagent, and take away food shop.

Fort Hommet

Between the southern end of Côbo Bay and Vazon Bay, the red granite of the **Hommet Peninsula** juts out into the sea. Fort Hommet is about 200 years old but its ruined barracks were demolished in 1955 after becoming dangerous. In 1982, a considerable amount of restoration work was undertaken on the remaining fabric of the fort, and as a result its appearance has been vastly improved.

The Germans did a considerable amount of work here, and today you can visit one of the bunkers which has been restored and refurbished. It contains an original 10.5cm gun. The fort's tower is a true Martello tower, whereas the other standing close-by is not. A comparison will reveal some important and obvious differences. As with many Guernsey forts, you are free to wander round without formality.

Close to the fort, a short distance to the north, there is a creek which is full of deep water at high-tide but, if you search carefully enough at low-tide, you'll find a cave 'Le Creux des Fées' (the fairy cave). There is plenty of parking on the headland.

Vazon Bay

South of the Hommet Peninsula lies Vazon Bay. This is one of the largest and most popular of Guernsey's beaches. On a rising tide, it is particularly appreciated by surfers who have an area specially reserved for them. Given the right wind, this beach can offer conditions as exciting as any beach in the UK. It is popular too with boardsailors and shore fishermen. Bass, mullet and plaice are often landed here.

Vazon is also the location for beach racing on eight Saturdays each summer. In addition, the road is closed on three occasions each year for sprint meetings when cars and motorcycles race against the clock. The slight curve in the road, adds to the excitement of the event.

There are beach kiosks at both ends of Vazon beach. The beach at **Richmond** in the south west of the bay, is probably the least popular. It is muddy at low water and there are sharp broken stones underfoot.

Inland

Le Guet

Inland from Côbo, Le Guet is worth a visit. This distinctive wooded hill was formerly owned by the de Saumarez family but now belongs to the States. At the summit there is a watch-house and gun battery built to give warning of French attack. There was also a beacon kept here to be lit if the enemy was sighted. In 1939, an air raid siren was installed here and it was sounded in 1940 when the Germans bombed the Island. Strangely though, folklore has it that the 'all clear' was never sounded.

The watch-house is closed to the public these days, but you can stand beside it and gain a good impression of the vast panoramic view which it commands. Below the watch-tower, there is a quarry and a powder magazine, and all around the hill there is evidence of German defence works.

Saumarez Park

Further inland from Côbo, Saumarez Park offers a pleasant alternative to seascapes. This estate was formerly the country house of the de Saumarez family whose generations lived there for over 200 years. Previously it had belonged to the Le Marchants, changing hands through inheritance. The arms of both families can be seen over one of the entrance gates.

The park has something to offer everyone:- a magnificent collection of mature trees, formal rose gardens and a small lake with ducks, as well as swings and an adventure playground. This is the largest park in the island and it hosts the annual **Battle of Flowers** which is the highlight of the **North Show**, one of two agricultural and horticultural shows held here each summer.

Saumarez House

Saumarez House was considerably enlarged during the early part of the twentieth century. At one time, when the fourth baron was in the Diplomatic Service, there were Japanese buildings erected here, built by Japanese workmen to ensure authenticity. He also had an attractive bridge built crossing the **Route de Carteret,** linking the park with **Mare de Carteret,** a neighbouring property.

While he was abroad, the house was used to provide accommodation for the Lieutenant Governor. At the time, Guernsey had no official Government House. Lord de Saumarez died in 1937, two years after he had entertained Edward, the Prince of Wales here. Following his death, the property was purchased by the States of Guernsey. During the occupation, it was used as States Offices.

The Guernsey Folk Museum

The Guernsey Folk Museum adjoins the residence. It is managed by the National Trust for Guernsey and the Societe Guernesiaise. The exhibits here concentrate upon rural Guernsey life of times past. Among other exhibits, the museum has a collection of old farm vehicles, a traditional cider press, and a reconstructed Guernsey kitchen. Saumarez Park is easily reached by bus from St Peter Port (2, 3A). Alternatively, there is ample car parking within the grounds. Refreshments are available.

Close by on the main road leading back to St Peter Port, there is a **Telephone Museum** which traces the history of the telephone in Guernsey since its introduction in 1898.

Walk from Saumarez to Côbo Bay

From Saumarez park it is a pleasant walk to Côbo Bay and Les Grande Rocques. Leave the park by the main gates on Côbo Road and pass the estate of **Le Pouquelah** on the right. Turn right along **Ruette de Saumarez** and go straight ahead onto **Ruette de la Tour** by the house called **Manor View**. There are fields on the left of this pleasant country lane and, on the right, there are views of Côbo. Soon you'll see a tower, a 'folly' belonging to the Saumarez estate. By the tower, follow the bridle path which gradually winds downhill and enter a world of trees, shrubs, old walls and quarries. There are plenty of seats along the route as well as a picnic area.

The path emerges on to **Route des Carteret** where the Saumerez footbridge crosses the road. Use the bridge and then follow the path past **Marie de Carteret School.** At the tennis courts, bear left after crossing the canal and then follow the track to the **Coast Road**. From here, Les Grandes Rocques and public transport are not far away.

St Saviour

Perelle Bay

Two parishes make up the central portion of Guernsey. St Saviour lies immediately south of Castel 'owning' the Perelle Bay portion of the western shoreline. This can be reached by bus from St Peter Port (7 and 7A). It is a rocky place, not particularly suited for sunbathing, but fascinating for naturalists or anyone with an interest in marine biology. Close by, there is '**Le Tricoteur'**, the only factory manufacturing Guernsey Sweaters on the Island. You can visit, watch the manufacturing process, and purchase a finished product from the factory shop – (VAT free of course).

Le Trepied

At the southern end of Perelle Bay, by some German defence works, there is **Le Trepied Dolmen,** a much quieter spot today than in the seventeenth century when it was believed to be a gathering place for practitioners of the black arts. This was the home of witches, some say perhaps even the devil himself. Even two hundred years later the area was still avoided by 'respectable' women. The dolmen was excavated in the nineteenth century by Frederick Lukis who discovered bones, arrowheads and fragments of beakers there. Today the finds are contained within the collection at the **Guernsey Museum.** Offshore, there is a tiny islet known as **Dom Hue,** where a hermit once lived.

The Chapel of St Apolline

No visit to Perelle Bay can be complete without seeing the chantry chapel of St Apolline, You'll find it about $^1/_4$ mile inland just a short distance along the shore. Turn inland at **Les Rouvets** and it is located on the left side of **La Grande Rue**, the main road. It was built in 1392 but later became used as a stable. It became the Island's first designated and protected 'ancient monument' when the States of Guernsey acquired it 1873. It was restored in 1980 and today it is still occasionally used for church services. Inside, there are traces of a fourteenth century fresco depicting the Last Supper. The furnishings are simple but appropriate.

Le Trepeid Dolmen

The Chapel of St Apolline

The Parish Church of St Saviour

Further inland from Perelle Bay, the Parish Church of St Saviour claims to be the largest of Guernsey's parish churches. It is a beautiful building which has a French style of architecture and craftsmanship. In the church yard there is a 'christianised' menhir, an ancient standing stone on which a deeply incised cross has been carved. There is also a gravestone marking the burial place of those lost when the cutter *'Pitt'* sank in Perelle Bay in 1819.

The church **spire** reaches 31m (103ft) and is topped with a weathercock. It makes a very distinctive landmark and point of reference for anyone walking the lanes around here. There are very few signposts. After all, most Guernsey folk know where they are so they don't need them. For the rest of us though, the spire can be seen from quite a distance and if you get lost you can always head back towards it, so the spire is a particularly useful point of reference.

The lanes round about the church are well worth visiting. This is a beautiful part of the Island, noted for its fine old farmhouses and outbuildings. Look out for the beautiful granite archways, the steps and blocks built into the walls along the roadside for mounting and dismounting horses, and the large stones and pebbles incorporated into the bases of buildings to stop carriage wheels scraping against them.

Guernsey Cattle: a Golden Breed

 You'll see them throughout the Island, roaming in the tiny fields, or more likely tethered by the roadside or on common ground. Guernsey cattle, like the Jersey breed, are world famous for their **good looks and rich milk**.

The breed was begun in about 960 A.D when Guernsey came to the attention of Robert, Duke of Normandy. He sent a group of militant monks to educate the natives, cultivate the soil and defend the Island. The monks brought with them the best bloodlines of French cattle – 'Norman Brindles', also known as 'Alderneys', from the province of Isigny, and the famous 'Froment du Leon' breed from Brittany. It was these two breeds which led to the development of the Guernsey cattle which we recognise today.

Originally, Guernseys were bred for their meat and they were frequently used as draught animals. During the eighteenth and nineteenth centuries however, they became better known for their milk which made a very rich butter. As their reputation grew, they were sent in thousands to Britain and in the 1840's they were even exported to America. The first were taken there by Captain Belair of the Schooner *Pilot*. Later, a certain Captain Prince imported two heifers and a bull from the Island. These animals are the origins of today's huge Guernsey herd in the USA.

As the Guernsey herd developed its own reputation and characteristics, importation of cattle from France was discontinued. Later, in order to maintain purity of the breed, imports of cattle from the UK were stopped, and in 1819 the importation of cattle from Jersey was made illegal.

In times past, Guernsey cattle were an ideal breed for the Island. They were good grazers, requiring very little land. A Guernsey cow produces milk with a high butterfat and protein content, but being of intermediate size, she consumes 20 to 30 percent less feed per pound of milk produced than do larger dairy breeds.

This was an important quality in Guernsey, where the old feudal system of government encouraged the division and fragmentation of land between members of a family as ownership passed from generation to generation.

The result has been a traditional system of **tethering** the Guernseys in small fields, and milking them where they stand. This practice is fast disappearing today, although you'll still see plenty of tethered animals around and about.

Compared with Jersey cattle, the Guernsey is a bigger and more solid animal. Both are golden in colour, although Guernseys often have white patches. Both breeds have something in common however, their **bulls are short tempered** and are among the most dangerous in the world. Over the years, many Jersey and Guernsey cattlemen have been killed by them.

St Saviour's Tunnel

During the Second World War, the spire was used as an observation post by the Germans, who also dug extensive tunnels under the foundations. After the war, a vast range of captured German military equipment was stored here by the British Army. St Saviour's Tunnel is open to the public and the entrance is at **Sous l'Eglise**, at the bottom of the hill on which the church stands.

Walk from St Saviour's to Perelle Bay

The walk from the church to the coast is very interesting. Begin by walking down the hill towards the **Tunnel Museum** and then from **Sous l'Eglise** follow **Rue l'Eglise** to the crossroads and turn right. Quite soon you'll reach the reservoir which is in fact a flooded valley. At times of drought, the remains of abandoned buildings in the valley can occasionally be seen breaking the surface of the waters.

From here climb **Rue du Moulin** to reach the main road and then turn left, downhill passing **Mont Varouf School.** Soon, on the left, you'll discover the approach to the massive **dam** built in 1947 which holds back 240 million gallons of water. There is a footpath across the dam and a track around the reservoir's perimeter.

On the far side of the dam turn right and right again to reach **Le Mont Saint, (Holy Hill)** reputed to be inhabited by fairies. From here there is a road running west to **Richmond** at the northern end of **Perelle Bay**. On the headland is Fort Richmond which overlooks Vazon Bay. Below there is another fort, **Fort Le Crocq,** which is privately owned. On the north side stands **Le Longue Pierre,** a menhir 3m (9ft) tall. A similar smaller stone stands nearby.

Places of interest

Just a short way to the south of the church at **Le Gron** are the gold and silver workshops of Bruce Russell and Son, housed in farm buildings dating from 1520. The company produces both traditional and modern jewellery. Admission to the workshops is free and there are demonstrations of the craft at 10.45 am each weekday morning. There is also a restaurant and a children's playground.

At **Les Issues,** the **Strawberry Farm** offers a huge range of shops to browse, the chance to paint your own pottery or sample home-made fudge from the fudge kitchens. There is also a children's play area, crazy golf, bumper boats and bumper cars, and a fully licensed restaurant with 'all you can eat nights' and entertainment.

Just adjacent, in the workshops of **Guernsey Woodcarvers**, you can watch the proprietor, John Le Messurier, design and build furniture. You can also see craftsmen French polishing items and turning bowls, lamps, and a variety of other items from over sixty different species of wood.

Kings Mills

One of the most pleasant spots in St Saviour's is Kings Mills which was described briefly in the Parish of Castel chapter. You can walk there from St Saviour's Church or alternatively buses from St Peter Port will get you there (Route 5A). The place gained its name from the water-mills which used to be located here, fed by the stream which runs through **Talbot Valley**.

Today, Kings Mills is the closest you'll get to a 'village' in the Island. There is no pub or church, but nonetheless it is a beautiful place with several old granite buildings set against a background of sheltering hills.

Kings Mills is a handy starting point for a visit to Talbot Valley or, alternatively, a walk to Vazon Bay. Simply walk westwards and take the second turning right after passing the **Hotel Fleur du Jardin**. A track will take you across **La Grande Mare**, an expanse of flat coutryside which was once a marsh. From here Vazon Bay, and buses back to St Peter Port are only a short distance away.

St Andrew's

This is the only parish without access to the sea. It is bordered by St Saviour and Castel to the west, St Peter Port and St Martin to the east, and Forest and St Peter in the Wood to the South. Despite its lack of beaches however, it still has a great deal to offer.

Churches

The Parish Church of St Andrew's is small and, although undated, it is clearly very old indeed. Of all the parish churches, this one most resembles an English parish church.

The Underground Military Hospital

During the occupation, the Germans chose St Andrew's as the location for their Underground Military Hospital. You'll find it in **La Vassalerie Road** close-by the St Andrew's Hotel. This is the largest construction in the Channel Islands. The network of tunnels, chambers and ventilation shafts were hewn out of solid rock by slaveworkers of many different nationalities. Many did not live to see the work completed and at the entrance to the museum, a section of unfinished tunnel gives an insight into the hardships they faced in the task they undertook.

The hospital had a kitchen, an operating theatre, an X-ray room, wards, storerooms and a mortuary, as well as staff quarters, a dispensary and a laboratory. It is said that after D-day, patients taken there from the battlefields of France were white as sheets after six weeks underground.

The hospital really cannot be described as an 'attraction' in the usual sense. It is, however, an important and moving reminder of Guernsey and Europe's past.

The popular Strawberry Farm has many craft workshops

THE VARIETY USED IS MAINLY RED GAUNTLET. GAUNTLET ONCE IT HAS FRUITED CAN BE CUT BACK, CLEANED UP A 'D WILL GIVE A FURTHER FLUSH OF BERRIES.

PLANTS AND BAGS ARE KEPT FOR 2 YEARS. HALF THE GREENHOUSES ARE REPLANTED EACH YEAR GIVING A MIX OF 1st AND 2nd YEAR PLANTS.

PLANTING COMMENCES IN OCTOBER WITH RUNNERS BOUGHT IN FROM THE MAINLAND FROM DISEASE-FREE STOCK. THE AUTUMN PLANTINGS GIVES THE PLANTS A MONTH OR SO TO ROOT BEFORE THEY GO DORMANT FOR THE WINTER.

IN SPRING WHEN GROWING STARTS THEY ARE FED WITH A LIQUID FEED THROUGH THE IRRIGATION SYSTEM OF 9-6-9. WHEN BERRIES HAVE FORMED THE FEED IS CHANGED TO A HIGH POTASH 3-6-12.

POLLINATION IS BY DOMESTIC BEES - THE HIVES ARE SITUATED BETWEEN EACH HOUSE.

ALTHOUGH THE METHOD OF SUSPENDING THE STRAWBERRIES GIVES A SLIGHTLY LOWER YIELD PER PLANT, THIS IS OFFSET BY THE 2 MAIN ADVANTAGES:-
1. A HIGHER QUALITY CLEANER CROP AND
2. THE EASE OF HARVESTING.

STRAWBERRIES HAVE BEEN GROWN AT THE FARM SINCE 1971. PRIOR TO THAT IT WAS TOMATOES.

DUE TO THE UNCERTAINTY OF GROWING IN GUERNSEY AROUND THE TIME WHEN BRITAIN ENTERED THE COMMON MARKET STRAWBERRIES WERE TRIED AS AN ALTERNATIVE CROP.

ORIGINALLY THE FRUIT WAS SOLD TO WHOLE-SALERS, HOTELS AND EXPORTED. NOW THE WHOLE CROP IS GIVEN OVER TO SUPPLYING VISITORS.

BEFORE THE OIL CRISIS OF 1976 THE CROP WAS HEATED - WHICH GAVE FRUIT FOR 9 MONTHS OF THE YEAR. NOW WITH THE PROHIBITIVE COST OF OIL AND CHEAP IMPORTS WORLDWIDE IT HAS BECOME UNECONOMICAL TO HEAT.

THE CROP IS NOW GROWN COLD. PICKING COMMENCES IN MAY THROUGH TO OCTOBER. EACH GREENHOUSE IS 150' LONG BY 30' WIDE. THERE ARE 300 GROW-BAGS PER HOUSE. EACH BAG HAS 3 ROWS OF 10 PLANTS - 30 IN ALL. SO ROUGHLY THERE ARE 9,000 PLANTS PER HOUSE. ON THE NURSERY AS A WHOLE THERE ARE 54,000 PLANTS.

Watch pottery being hand-made at the Strawberry Farm

The small church of St Andrews dates from the 12th century

Another church, the **Little Chapel** of **Les Vauxbelets,** stands less than half a mile away however, and this tends to attract far more interest than the parish church.

The Little Chapel was built in 1923 by Brother Deodat and Brother Cephas, French monks from a religious house which administered the school and farm in the large and attractive estate of Les Vauxbelets. The Chapel, modelled on the shrine at Lourdes, is made almost entirely of fragments of china pottery and sea shells. At only 16ft in length it claims to be the smallest church in the world.

Building the church was Brother Deodat's life's work. This chapel was, in fact, his third attempt. The first one which he commenced in 1914, was criticised and so he destroyed it. The second, although a perfect replica of the Lourdes shrine, was also demolished when it proved to be too small to enable the bishop to enter and consecrate it.

After his third attempt, Brother Deodat returned to France where he died shortly after the end of the Second World War. The Brothers still bring parties of French school children to visit Les Vauxbelets.

Places of interest

Further along the track leading to the Little Chapel, **Guernsey Clockmakers** have their workshops where you can see clocks and barometers being made.

St Andrew's is also the parish where you'll find one of the best known and prestigious hotels in the Island. The **St Pierre Park**, situated at the foot of **Rohais Road**, is built on the site of a former Roman Catholic school. It stands in 40 acres of parkland and landscaped grounds which includes a nine-hole golf course.

Channel Islands' Legends

Isolated communities are always a good source of folk history tales, passed down from generation to generation, sometimes fantastically improbable, but usually with a grain of truth somewhere within the rich weave of the story. Fishermen too, at the mercy of the weather for their livelihood and safety, also tend to rely upon close observation of nature and other 'signs' to indicate their luck and warn them of danger.

Put the two elements together on an island and you have a recipe for a community which pays great heed to folklore and superstition. Perhaps that is why there are so many locations in the Islands which used to be accredited as the haunts of fairies. It is interesting to note that Channel Island fairies were not always 'good'. Even less than one hundred years ago in Guernsey, there were fairy rings and other locations of which Islanders steered well clear.

Such superstition probably accounts for why the Islands' history is also steeped in a belief in **witches and witchcraft**. Guernsey, for example, has the unenviable reputation of having convicted on average one witch per year for 150 years, while England, with a much greater population, convicted only 2,000 during the same period. The last witchcraft trial in Guernsey took place in January 1914 and resulted in Amy Henrietta Queripel being sentenced to eight days' hard labour.

But it wasn't only witches who brought bad luck. In days gone by, people believed in other signs too. Take, for example, the story of the man who decided to demolish **La Rocque qui Sonne** (the singing rock). Everyone warned him that evil befell anyone who attempted to damage it, but he took no heed. So little credit did he give the old superstition that he even included some of the pieces of the shattered rock in the foundations of the new house he was building.

Unfortunately, the house burned down before he could move in and two servants died in the blaze. He shipped some of the stone to England in two vessels and both of them sank. He moved to Alderney, but his house burned down there also. Finally, he sailed back to Guernsey, but en route some of the ship's rigging fell on his head and killed him.

Mixed marriages were also considered to be a poor omen and probably doomed to failure. How could any good come from a marriage to a Jersey man or woman!

Jersey people were held in such contempt by Guernsey Islanders, that they were referred to as **toads**. Neither do Guernsey people seem to have had a great deal of time for people of other Islands. Alderney folk were known as **cows**, while Islanders from Sark were **crows**.

Guernsey folk even had nicknames for each other, depending upon which parish they came from. Castel and Torteval folk were **donkeys,** Forest folk were **drones**. People from St Martin's were **ray fish**, those from St Peter in the Woods were **beetles**, and parishioners of St Saviour's were **ants.** Vale folk were **cockchafers**.

6 Southern Parishes

ST PETER IN THE WOODS

St Peter in the Woods (sometimes referred to as St Pierre du Bois) and Torteval are the two south western parishes of the Island and many people consider them to be the most beautiful. Certainly there has been less 'development' here – the landscape and scenery remains much as it was a hundred years ago.

They also have a variety of landscapes to offer. There are low-lying shores and broad sandy bays, as elsewhere, but there are also majestic cliffs, secluded coves, hidden caves, wooded valleys and a wide range of views, from pastoral scenes to high clifftop panoramas. Given the right weather, you'll find everything here, from gentle countryside scenes to the drama of a storm-tossed sea exploding in a welter of foam over reefs and off-lying rocks. For these reasons, St Peter and Torteval feature large in many visitors' itineraries.

St Peter in the Woods' coastline runs roughly from **Le Trepied Dolmen** in the north to the **Brock Battery** in **Rocquaine Bay** to the south. In effect, the greater part of Rocquaine Bay belongs to this parish.

Opposite page: Forest parish church

Below: Crab pots at L'Erée

Left: Fort Saumarez Observation Tower on Lihou Headland

L'Erée

The northern headland of L'Erée really must be visited. You can get within walking distance of the headland by public transport (bus 7 & 7A), and there is also ample car parking.

From the main coast road take the small road leading to the headland, and as you climb the hill leading to the massive German tower, look out for a small inconspicuous turning on the right. This is the entrance to **Le Creux ès Faies**, a small mound with the entrance to a dolmen beneath it. Folklore has it that this is the entrance to fairyland. There are still some older Guernsey people who will not approach it, especially at night if there is a full moon!

It is, in fact, a long tomb which you can enter and explore – similar to the Déhus Dolmen in Vale parish – but it is considerably smaller and so no artificial light is required. Excavations suggest that it is about 4,000 year old, in use between 2,000 and 1800 BC. Beaker pottery was found here which is now on display at the Guernsey Museum.

The German tower beyond Le Creux ès Faies was built upon the older **Fort Saumarez**. **L'Erée Headland** is an ideal spot from which to take in the views south-wards along the broad sweep of Rocquaine Bay, and northwards towards Les Grandes Rocques.

Immediately to seawards is the **Isle of Lihou** which is easy to reach for a couple of hours on foot at low tide. There is a partially-paved causeway which winds over the rocky shore and threads its way between numerous rock pools to reach the Island. It was probably constructed by the monks who built a priory here in earlier times.

Lihou

This island is about half a mile in length and has an area of approximately eighteen acres. Usually, there is a board on the island which advises visitors of the time to leave before the tide covers the causeway, but in any case, never attempt to cross either way if any part of the causeway has water over it. The rock pools fill very quickly and once the causeway is covered, a savage current flows between the isle and the headland. In effect, if the tide returns while you are on Lihou, you'll have to remain there for about eleven hours until the causeway uncovers again.

Lihou is a quiet spot well worth a visit, especially if you enjoy birdwatching or just basking in the sun and taking in the peace and tranquillity of the place. There are two deep rockpools in the west of the island which are ideal for swimming.

The original farmhouse on the island was destroyed by the Germans when they used it as a target for their battery of guns on the headland. Close by, there was also a small factory for the production of **iodine** made from dried seaweed collected from the beach. This too was destroyed by the occupying forces.

In the early 1970's the buildings were restored by Lt-Col. P.A. Wootten, who opened the island to the public with summer camps for young people (**Lihou Youth Project**) to encourage them to develop a Christian outlook. One post-war tenant also introduced sheep which became accustomed to eating "**Vraic**" (seaweed), possibly due to the fact that little else grew.

Later it was occupied by Crown

tenants, Robin and Mrs Borwick. Now however, it is the property of 'The States of Guernsey' and a report was published in 1996 as to the future use of the island. One popular idea is to use the island to encourage schools and other groups to undertake environmental studies here.

St Mary's Priory

Also on Lihou, there are some remains of St Mary's Priory, built by Benedictine Monks in the year 1114. It was originally under the control of the Abbey of Mont St Michel and occupied by Benedictine monks, one of whom, Brother Jean de L'Espin, was murdered by the Prior's servant Thomas Le Roser in 1299. The prior was fined '100 sols Tournis' for permitting such a thing to happen. The priory was sequestrated and given over to Eton College in 1415 after which it appears to have failed altogether. It fell into ruin during the reformation and was destroyed by neglect, wind and weather. German guns had nothing to do with its present condition.

Further away over the reefs there is a smaller islet called **Lihoumel**. Visitors returning from here some times say that they feel they have been to the edge of the world. If you are looking for solitude, here's the place.

Rocquaine Bay

Travelling south from L'Erée Headland, the road runs along Rocquaine Bay towards **Fort Grey**. This bay has the highest section of sea wall in the island. It was built to prevent coastal erosion and was reinforced by the Germans during the occupation. It stands 40ft tall in places and offers good protection from the wind for anyone using the beach.

Half-way along the road stands **Le Rocque Poisson** (Fish Rock), a large rock which is a prominent feature on the seawards side of the road. A short distance further on there is **Brock Battery**, yet another of the Island's numerous defences against a French invasion. A lane runs inland from here, rising to **La Route des Paysanes**.

Places of interest

Continue up the hill and, on the right just before the summit, there is a standing stone in the middle of a privately owned field. This is **La Longue Rocque,** the tallest menhir in Guernsey. According to legend, it was once a cricket bat used by the fairies. Another older tale suggests that it was brought here by a fairy woman who carried it from the shore in her apron. Some apron! Some fairy! The stone is at least 3.5m (11.5ft) tall and its weight can only be guessed at.

A half mile further along this road, after a right turn at the Longfrie Hotel, you'll find the **Parish Church of St Peter's.** This is an ancient church indeed, mentioned in a charter of the year 1030. It was built on a wooded hill-side rather than at the summit, so you may fail to notice the height of the church tower which stands at 33m (over 100ft). When you enter the church however, you'll notice a pronounced upward slope of the floor from west to east. Look out for the beautiful tower arch and the rose window above it. At the northern entrance gate, there is a mounting block from the days when some of the congregation might have arrived on horseback. The war memorial is located to the east of the church.

Close by the church, the **Coach House Gallery**, which recently won a Civic Trust award, is well worth visiting. As well as containing permanent exhibitions of the works of resident artists Maria Whinney and Barry Owen Jones, you may also find works by non-Guernsey artists – sculptures by James Butler, watercolours by Vivian Pitchforth, and bronzes by Nenne van Dijk. Works of Sir Hugh Casson have also been exhibited here.

TORTEVAL

From Brock Battery southwards along the Coast Road, you are in the Parish of Torteval. Inland, from the Torteval coast, the pointed spire of the Parish Church is a highly recognisable landmark. The church itself is not so beautiful as its neighbours. It is a relatively modern building, constructed in 1816 as a replacement for an older church which had fallen into poor condition. Some say the earlier church was much more beautiful than its modern replacement. Despite its modernity, **Torteval Church** is the custodian of the oldest bell in the island, cast in 1432.

Fort Grey

Back on the coast, just over the parish boundary is Fort Grey with its distinctive whitewashed Martello tower. Originally, it was known as the **Chateau de Rocquaine**, reputedly

Torteval church

a haunt of witches. The old fort was rebuilt in 1804 as a defence against French attack, and was renamed 'Grey' after a Lieutenant Governor of the Island.

In 1976, Fort Grey was opened as a **Maritime Museum** specialising in recording Island shipwrecks. Here you'll find artefacts and pictures recording a large number of marine disasters, including modern wreckings such as the *Prosperity* which scattered building timber all along the west coast, the *Elwood Mead* which met disaster on her maiden voyage carrying iron ore from Australia, and the oil rig *Orion*, who broke her tow ropes and ran aground at **Les Grandes Rocks** just to the north of here. Fort Grey offers shelter to a number of small fishing boats which

Fort Grey and the Shipwreck Museum

have moorings here and is a pleasant spot to visit.

Guernsey Copper Craft stands opposite Fort Grey. It has a fine range of brass and copperware on sale and it has a cafe. Just north of here, a road runs inland to the **Coach House Gallery**, but if you continue south along the Coast Road, you'll arrive at the headland known as Pleinmont.

Pleinmont

The little harbour of **Portelet** on the northern side of this headland is well worth a visit. It is overlooked by the Trinity House cottages, traditionally occupied by the lighthouse keepers and their families. It was from Portelet that they were ferried in a Trinity House launch to and from the **Les Hanois** lighthouse which stands a couple of miles out to sea from **Pleinmont Point**. The lighthouse was constructed in 1862. Travelling in a straight line, after Pleinmont and the lighthouse, the next land you'll encounter is the continent of America. The lighthouse today has been automated. There are no keepers permanently stationed there any more.

The lane running up to the **Torteval Heights** from Portelet is known as 'the zigzag'. It leads up to the television masts and the old German artillery direction finding tower which stand above the point. The five-storey tower has been re-equipped and is open to the public each Sunday 2-5pm April to October inclusive.

Further west from Portelet you'll find **Fort Pézéries**, an eighteenth century construction, built on the site of a much older work. The Fort has been well preserved and the gun emplacements and magazines are intact. For defence purposes its location was well chosen. Its guns could be trained on anyone attempting a landing in Rocquaine Bay, and it was itself well protected from seaward attack by the rocks and the raging currents which sweep around them. There is plenty of car parking within walking distance of both Portelet and Fort Pézéries.

At **Pleinmont Point,** the cliff comes to an end and the path takes you down to a grassy spot surrounded by rocky heights, a gap in the rock then takes you further towards the 'lands-end' of Guernsey. There is a slipway here, which was used by farmers to collect seaweed from the beach. **'Vraic',** (pronounced 'rack') as it is called, was used as a form of fertiliser. The farmers brought it up the slipway in carts pulled by heavy horses and spread it over the fields each autumn.

At Pleinmont Point you'll find an old watch-tower which is said to have been used by Victor Hugo as the setting for the 'haunted house' in his book *The Toilers of the Sea.*

The South Coast

Continuing our anticlockwise tour around the Island, your direction from L'Ancresse in the north of the Island would have been southwards. From now on however, you'll be travelling east-wards along the south coast. The main road here is higher than elsewhere, and it runs some distance inland from the sea. From now on, visits to the coast are made as detours, often descending steeply through wooded valleys to small isolated rocky coves. Here, the wide views are gone in favour of smaller, more intimate glimpses of sea and coastline.

Walk from Les Tielles to Pleinmont

For the walker however, there are still opportunities to remain close to the sea. There are sixteen miles of cliff path along the south coast from St Peter Port to Pleinmont. The section from Les Tielles to Pleinmont is particularly interesting, but before you undertake it, read the notes on walking Guernsey's cliff paths (see page 119).

The best time to undertake the Les Tielles to Pleinmont section of the cliff path walk is in early summer. The flowers and vegetation are at their best then. At Les Tielles you'll find the path close by the Martello tower. Walking westwards from here, you'll arrive at **Mont Herault Watch House**. It is in fact just a cottage, but its location gives it a sort of grandeur which makes it conspicuous from a distance although less so at close-quarters.

From here there is a track down the cliffside to the tiny inlet of **Belle Elizabeth**, named, so legend has it, after a young girl who plunged to her death here, because her parents had forbidden her to marry her lover. There is a rock just offshore which is said to be the girl, petrified in stone for all eternity.

Further west, there is a shallow valley near Mont Herault where a path will take you down to **Baie de la Forge**, a wild and savage cove in which you'll find a 'souffleur', otherwise known as a blow-hole. The best time to see it in action is about two hours after low water on a sunny day. Then the sea, forced into a small opening in the rock, forces air and spray out through the blow-hole above. On a good day, you'll find columns of spray shooting out through the hole, and turning into rainbows in the sunlight. The souffleur makes plenty of noise too. You can get down to the floor of the bay from here but it is a steep decent and a strenuous climb back.

Further along the cliff path you'll arrive at **La Congrelle**, roughly translated as 'the place of the congers,' a name which would create a very dramatic image for anyone familiar with this creature: the conger eel is perhaps the most powerful, malevolent and feared catch of any fisherman in Channel Island waters.

There are plenty of stories about the viciousness of congers hauled up from the depths and brought aboard small boats, so the idea of visiting a location where they might be encountered in some strength, may not appeal to all. But despite its name, visiting this high-sided, water-filled gully is worth the effort.

From below, the cliffs are dark and sheer and the German tower standing on the heights of **L'Angle** look particularly menacing. **Gull Rock**, a stack towering out of the sea, also adds to the drama of the place. You won't find a gentle picture postcard image of Guernsey here. This is something more primitive and raw, a severe beauty which, in some respects, is more enduring and truthful.

Further west along the path, the Television Masts of Pleinmount appear alongside the German artillery direction-finding tower, and then out to sea you can obtain a good view of **Les Hanois Lighthouse**.

Sausmarez Manor

Guernsey's only stately home, Sausmarez Manor is located within St Martin's parish. On certain days it is open to the public, but even on 'closed' days, the grounds are worth a visit.

A house stood on this site in the thirteenth century and fragments of it still survive, but the house you see today dates from the reign of Queen Anne. The Island's most ancient family, the de Sausmarez family, lived here up to 1557 when the property passed into the hands of the Andros family. Sir Edmund Andros, who was the Bailiff and Lieutenant-Governor of the Island and Governor of Massachusetts and New York, designed the facade.

John de Sausmarez bought the house back in 1749, using part of a fortune amassed and left to him by his brother Philip, captain of the 'Centurion'. The entrance gates to the property, with their greyhound and unicorn emblems, mark the event.

Today, on special occasions when members of the family gather in the dining room, they are surrounded by portraits of family members spanning several centuries.

Inside the house, among the many exhibits you'll find the wedding suit of King James II. The estate also houses the third largest **Dolls House Collection** in Britain. It is maintained within a Tudor barn and has exhibits dating back to 1830.

The grounds include a wild sub-tropical garden, and spaces devoted to pitch and putt, petanque, and putting. There is also a 7.25 inch gauge railway which runs through the woodland estate. A number of charitable concerts and fetes are held here each year.

The **Sculpture Trail** is heralded as one of the most beautiful and comprehensive in Britain and includes work from many different countries.

Beside the estate's gate stands the court-house of the Fief de Sausmarez. Nearby at **Les Camps du Moulin**, on the road to **Le Vallon**, is the tower of the old manorial windmill.

FOREST PARISH

Travelling eastwards from Torteval, you briefly enter the Parish of St Peter in the Woods again before moving on to Forest, a tiny parish but with much to see. In fact, for many visitors, Forest is the first glimpse they get of the Island. The Airport was built here in 1939.

Places of Interest

Forest Parish Church is a good place to begin exploration. You can travel there by bus from St Peter Port (Bus 7 & 7A). It is the smallest parish church in the Island and, like most of the other parish churches, it is of great age. The eastern end is probably the oldest. Here you'll find an old 'piscina', where priests used to rinse their hands at mass. The small church tower has four bells, and probably one of the most consulted clocks in the Island. Travellers use it to check the time on the way to the airport. It was installed as a memorial of Queen Victoria's Diamond Jubilee. During the occupation, this church was closed because it was too near the airport for safety.

Near the church, the **German Occupation Museum** is well worth a visit. It began as a collection of wartime souvenirs gathered together by a group of schoolboy friends. The leader of the group, Richard Heaume, became so fascinated by German military artefacts that his ever-expanding collection soon could only be stored in a museum. Today, it is full of valuable and poignant reminders of the occupation. Among the exhibits there is a complete field kitchen discovered in the German tunnels in St Saviour, uniforms, helmets and gas masks, a life-sized street, bunker rooms and a cinema. The museum also has a cafe.

The South Coast

From here, there is a lane which, if followed far enough, will take you into **Petit Bôt Valley** by the Manor hotel. It is a delightful walk down to Petit Bôt, which is one of the most attractive of the south coast beaches. Bear in mind however, that it is a long climb back from there.

Petit Bôt Bay

At some point however, Petit Bôt Bay will need to be seen. There used to be two windmills here but the Germans destroyed them, afraid that they might be used by British troops or spies. Their fears were well founded. In 'Operation Ambassador', the first British commando raid of the Second World War, British troops landed at **Petit Port** just a few miles east of here.

Today, Petit Bôt Bay has no accommodation. There is a tiny cottage, an eighteenth century defence tower, and the remains of a mill and waterwheel. There is also a cafe which is popular with large numbers of tourists who value Petit Bôt for its beauty, its fine sand, and its sheltered sunbathing. It offers protection from the wind from all directions except south and it has to be one of the most beautiful spots in the Island.

A stream which runs down the valley and trickles across the beach marks the boundary between the parishes of Forest and St Martin. On the western side of Petit Bôt there is **Portelet Bay**. It is sandy and secluded but it can only be reached by footpath. At high tide, access to the beach is impossible. Car parking can be a problem at Petit Bôt, and the best advice is to arrive early.

An alternative to visiting Petit Bôt Bay is to turn right instead of left, and climb up to **Le Variouf**, a hamlet of great beauty. From there, you can continue to the coast at **Les Fontenelles** or **Le Gouffre** where there are caves and a restaurant. This part of the coast around the headland of **La Moye** is well known for its sometimes spectacularly savage seas. There is an attractive fishing harbour here.

Other bays

Westwards beyond Le Gouffre lies **La Corbière Point,** another place where you can sit down and enjoy extensive views to seaward and along the coast. As with most headlands there is a car park.

From here there is a good path down to **Harve de Bon Repos** (harbour of good rest) – living proof that Guernsey people have a well developed sense of humour. There are few places so uninviting to the skipper of a small boat. The rocks here would turn the strongest craft to matchwood within minutes. Despite this, Bon Repos has a small swimming pool so it can be a pleasant enough place, providing you keep a look out for falling rocks!

Walk from Le Bourg to St Martin's

Most travellers going eastwards from Forest towards the parish of St Martin's use the main road which links the airport and St Peter Port. It is busy and unattractive but there are alternative routes. You can walk, for example, to St Martin's village from Le Bourg by heading for **Le Chêne** traffic lights and then turning left. This road winds towards **Rue des Agneaux** which runs eastwards becoming **Le Chemin le Roi** at some stage. It passes the **Haut Nez**, a water tower standing on Guernsey's highest point 104m (342ft) above sea level.

Le Chemin le Roi joins a secondary road near **Les Mouilpieds**, a collection of fine old houses, and shortly afterwards, you'll rejoin the **Forest Road** at **Les Cornus**. From here St Martin's shopping centre is less than a half mile away. For most car drivers however, the best advice is to stay with the main Forest Road. It may be busy and unappealing, but it's also short!

ST MARTIN'S

St Martin's Parish Church

St Martin's Parish Church is close by the busy shopping centre and located only a couple of hundred yards from a very busy road, but it could just as well be miles away. It is a haven of peace set in beautiful surroundings and it really must be visited.

The ornate south porch is a fifteenth century design which used to be the

Petit Bôt Bay

Fermain Bay

Walking Guernsey's Cliff Path

There is a continuous **sixteen mile** cliff path from St Peter Port to Pleinmont, but to attempt the full distance in one day requires a great deal of stamina. Even experienced walkers find it hard. The distance is not so great, but there are many steep climbs and descents which make the route a tiring one. If you are not a regular walker, begin with fairly short treks along sections of the path until you gain the measure of what is required.

Public transport is the best way to get to the departure point for any planned cliff path walk. It is also a good idea to plan to end your walk somewhere near a bus route back to St Peter Port, preferably in a location where you can obtain refreshments while waiting for the bus.

The general state of the cliff path is good, but it is still important that you wear appropriate clothing and tough, comfortable shoes. It is also important that you take care on the cliff-tops and stay on the recognised path. Avoid climbing up or down in places where no obvious path exists.

Take care with matches and discarded cigarettes too. At certain times of year the vegetation can be 'tinder' dry, and fires on cliffsides can be notoriously difficult to put out.

Likewise, **leave no litter**: the beauty of the route can be easily spoiled by discarded drink cans and sandwich packets gleaming in the sunlight. There are cafes and toilets in most bays and at some viewpoints, but it is still a good idea to take some refreshments with you.

Sunblocker is useful too – there is little shade on the path and the cliffs are south facing, so you'll be in strong direct sunlight for most of the trip.

It is difficult to become lost on the coastal path, but a good *Ordnance Survey Map,* or a copy of *Perry's Guide Map,* is always useful. Finally, bearing in mind those steep ascents and descents, give yourself plenty of time to rest and take in the scenery – after all, you're on holiday.

meeting place for the parish authorities, but in 1869 the church was refurbished and the authorities were asked to find somewhere else to hold their meetings.

Inside, there are some interesting memorials. The **pulpit** was constructed in 1655 and, although the windows are quite modern, they are interesting and their design is sympathetic to the general age and beauty of the building. The well designed tower has three bells cast in 1736.

La Gran'mere du Chimquiere

At the church yard gate, there is a carved stone which at times has been described as both the 'oldest woman in Guernsey', and the 'finest carved menhir in Europe'. This remarkable piece of granite, known as **'La Gran'mere du Chimquiere'** (The Grandmother of the Cemetery), was probably a fertility goddess carved by Neolithic settlers in Guernsey. There are indications that she was remodelled and 'improved' around the time of Christ, when changes were made to her face, hair and head-dress. At sometime in the past also, someone attempted to cut the menhir in two but the toughness of the granite proved too much for the vandal.

Once again, we have yet another example of how the early Christians built their churches on ground which had been previously used by older religions. In this instance, it is almost certain that this was the site of an ancient cemetery. St Martin's Church dates back to the late twelfth or early

thirteenth centuries, but it replaced a much older wooden structure.

Today, La Gran'mere is a much respected figure! Traditionally, brides who marry in the church scatter flowers over her head or place a garland over her shoulders. Wedding parties often like to include La Gran'mere in their photographs too.

From the church, buses (7A) will get you to St Peter Port, a distance of only two miles, or it can be a pleasant walk to return down through the country lanes. Before you go anywhere however, make a point of strolling a couple of hundred yards along the road to look at the old houses and gardens in the tiny settlement of **La Bellieuse**. This is one of the most unspoiled and beautiful corners of the Island.

The East Coast

It is an easy walk from Sausmarez Manor (see next page) to Fermain Bay on the east coast, just south of St Peter Port. This is one of the most popular and attractive bays in the Island. From the manor gates walk left for a few yards and then take the turning right which follows **Le Varclin Valley.** When you reach **Calais Lane**, look out for the stone sign pointing to the cliff path which leads down to the bay.

Fermain Bay

You can walk there from **La Vallette** in St Peter Port. It is only 1.75 miles to Fermain from La Vallette. It is quite a strenuous walk over the cliffs but there are steps and plenty of seats en route and the views are tremendous. The trip is delightful and the destination is well worth seeing. If you are planning on driving however, bear in mind that you cannot drive right to the bay – you will need to park in **Rue du Putron** or **Becquet Road** off the **Fort Road**, and then walk down from there. You can go down to the bay to drop off disabled passengers with a permit from ☎ (01481) 243400 (Mr Phil Ogier).

Once on the beach, you'll notice the huge sea wall topped by a defensive tower built here to discourage invasion. Both of these defences are overlooked by a napoleonic sentry box mounted on the hillside. For reasons which will be obvious to you when you see it, locals call it 'the pepper pot'. The stream coming down **Fermain Valley** marks the boundary between the parishes of St Martin and St Peter Port. Fermain Bay can hardly be described as a sandy beach, in fact at high water there is no sand to be seen at all. Fermain also has the reputation of having the coldest sea water in Guernsey.

Despite this, it is a very popular location and so well sheltered that it can become a suntrap on clear sunny days. There are refreshments here and usually floats to hire. The northern end of the bay is marked by concrete moorings which are rarely used by boats these days but they are popular with sunbathers and swimmers. Swimming and diving from the steps is excellent too.

On the right of Fermain Bay, reached by cliff path, is **Le Grande Creux,** a deep cave which is worth seeing. There is another, less impressive cave at the opposite end of the Bay.

The South Coast

But what about the other bays, coves, and headlands on the south coast which haven't been mentioned yet? Well, eastwards from Petit Bôt, there is **La Jaonnet**, a beautiful cove reached by footpath and steps from the cliff top. At low tide, you can walk along the beach here to **La Bétte Bay**, and on towards **Le Creux au Chien**, (the Dog's Cave.) Few people visit these little bays. Probably they are put off by the thought of the climb back to the clifftop, but if you value solitude and the simple pleasures of sunshine and clean sand, these are places well worth exploring.

East of Le Creux au Chien lies the magnificent headland of **Icart Point**. Public transport (Route 6 & 6A) can get you within half a mile of the point. There is a car park here together with refreshments.

Icart Point

At Icart, there are excellent views westwards towards Petit Bôt and the rugged Point de la Moye and eastwards across Saints Bay, Moulin Huet and Petit Port to the Pea Stacks and Jerbourg Point.

Below, the cliff slopes down to **La Petite Coupée**, a crumbling isthmus leading to a spur of rock which is now in so dangerous a state that it has been fenced off. From here the walk back to Petit Bôt along the cliff path is about two miles.

Saints' Bay

No one knows how Saints' Bay got its name, although some say that it is named after two rocks there which are

St Martin's parish church. At the entrance stands the prehistoric La Gran'mere du Chimquiere (great mother of the century), an ancient statue menhir

shaped like saints – I've never found them! You can get close to the bay by public transport (Route 6 & 6A), and from the top of the valley road where you alight, it is a pleasant walk along the country lane down to the beach.

On the way, you can also make a short detour, by taking a right turn down a narrow road which leads past a Martello tower and onwards to a tiny fishing harbour built during the last century, largely from money donated by the Seigneur of Blanchelande. When the Germans fortified this area, they threw the obelisk erected in memory of him onto the beach but after the war it was recovered and reinstated. At times, this tiny port can be spoiled by the weight of traffic. There are few parking places here, and only limited parking.

Moulin Huet Bay

East of Saints' Bay lies Moulin Huet Bay, a place which has achieved fame in verse and painting as an area of outstanding beauty. The French impressionist painter Pierre Auguste **Renoir** painted the bay eighteen times in 1883.

The approaches to the bay are beautiful also. Try following the cliff path eastwards from Saints Bay or westwards from Petit Port; neither of these routes are over a half mile in length, but the views and the scenery you'll encounter are magnificent. By road, you'll need to do a little walking from the bus stop, or the valley car park. Most people approach the bay through the hamlet of **La Ville Amphrey**.

Walking from the bus stop, you'll see the remains of the de Sausmarez Windmill on the left as you descend

Rupert The Bear

When the editor of the *Daily Express* decided to include a childrens' cartoon in his newspaper, he gave the task of devising the character and storyline to his deputy, a rather squat cigar-smoking journalist called **Herbert Tourtel**, a Guernseyman, born on 7th January 1874 and educated at Elizabeth College in St Peter Port.

By the time he was approached to produce the strip cartoon, he was already a published poet and his wife Mary was a skilled childrens' illustrator. He was sure that if she could devise the character, he could provide the story in rhyming couplets to match her illustrations. Rupert's first appearance was in a story entitled *Little Bear Lost,* published in the *Daily Express* on the 8th November 1920.

Despite his apparently simple appearance, Rupert has never been an easy bear to draw. The shape of the head and the positioning of the eyes are crucial features of the design which goes to make the 'Rupert' which we all recognise. Place the eye dots a shade too high or low, too close together or far apart, and you have a totally different bear – not Rupert at all! This difficulty has nearly been Rupert's downfall on several occasions.

Soon after Rupert's first appearance, Herbert Tourtel died. **Mary** continued to illustrate Rupert tales, working with a number of writers until 1935 when failing eyesight forced her to retire.

This could easily have been the end of Rupert Bear, had **Alfred Bestall** not decided to take up the challenge. He proved to be the ideal successor. He was of a much more modern school than Mary Tourtel and he was able to enlarge upon her original theme.

Under Bestall's direction, many new characters were introduced including The Conjurer, Tiger Lilly and the Three Girl Guides. Most important of all, Bestall worked hard to establish a definite form and geography to Rupert's home village of **Nutwood**. Up to this time it had been a rather vague location. Bestall succeeded in anchoring Rupert's adventures in a landscape which became familiar to readers, adding credibility to the tales and also offering readers an escape to a secure place at a time when the real world was moving towards the Second World War.

Today, Bestall's work sets the standard by which all 'Ruperts' are judged. The 'real' Rupert bear appears on every frame of a strip cartoon, and his check trousers have only six horizontal bands. Beware of impostors!

Rupert Collectables

At present, Rupert items are very 'collectable'. Jigsaws, miniature figures, badges, and of course *Daily Express Newspapers* containing episodes of his adventures, are all much sought after, but many collectors concentrate upon completing collections of **Rupert Annuals** which have been published each year since 1936.

Making a collection of Rupert items can be quite difficult. They were produced for children and so many show all the signs of rough treatment. It is very unusual to find an Annual in 'mint condition' with all pages intact and without a child's name written on the first page. Wartime annuals are the most difficult to find. They were produced in paperback, and only a small quality were printed.

Mary Tourtel didn't help the situation either. She had little love for the character she created, regretting the fact that she was not involved in 'more serious' art. As a result, despite having produced thousands of illustrations, no surviving original sketches have ever been discovered.

Rupert Stamps

In 1994 the Guernsey Post Office commemorated Rupert's links with the Island by producing a special series of postage stamps. They too have become collectors items**.** If you enjoy browsing through markets and bric-a-brac shops, you could still strike gold by finding an original Rupert illustration by Mary Tourtel. After all, if they exist anywhere, Guernsey is probably the first place to look!

to the Wishing Well at the head of **Water Lane**. From here there is a path which follows the stream down the valley. From the car park, it is an easy descent to the bay. There are refreshments here.

Another approach is to take the bus to **La Fosse** and walk down the beautiful wooded valley road past the **Moulin Huet Pottery,** a family business run by Rex Opie, his wife Robina and their daughter Karla. You can watch the potters at work or visit the studio above which sells stoneware, porcelain, paintings and limited edition prints.

The bay itself is very attractive with the massive **Cradle Rock** in the centre and the **Dog and Lion Rocks** away to the west. There is some sand at low water and many people, having climbed down the steps, make for the far end of the beach but this can only be reached when the tide permits and the return can be difficult. Swimming in the rock gullies is excellent.

Above the bay are the wooded grounds of **Le Vallon**, once the family seat of the Carey family. It isn't open to the public although it can be pleasant to walk there from the **Jerbourg Road**.

Petit Port Bay

This bay can be reached by public transport (Route 6 & 6A) and there is a long flight of steps which are easy enough to use on the way down, but promise an exhausting return climb at the end of the day. Once down, you'll find yourself in a delightful sheltered bay and often you'll have the place pretty much to yourself. At low tide there is a broad expanse of sand and in

the cliff faces there are caves to explore. One in particular has a 'creux', an opening in the roof. The surf can be exciting here too, given the right state of wind and tide.

Jerbourg Point

You can reach Jerbourg Point which marks the eastern end of Moulin Huet Bay, after a short walk from the bus stop (6 & 6A). There is a car park and refreshments are available on the headland. The seaward views from here are very wide. On a good day, you'll see Jersey to the south, the other Channel Islands to the east, and France on the horizon behind them.

From the point, you can see the **Peastacks**, the finest chain of rocks in the Channel Islands. From a boat however, they appear even more impressive. One of them is known as **Le Petit Bon Homme d'Andrilot** (The Good Little Man Named Andrew). In times past, fishermen used to doff their caps or lower their topsails in respect for him. At close quarters, from the deck of a small boat, he seems much more like a giant than a small man!

There is an excellent path around the headland at Jerbourg and, as you would expect, evidence of German defence works are everywhere, but there is an older gun battery at **Le Havre des Mois** in the shadow of the Peastacks. A path from here leads down to sea level. One German battery near the Peastacks, with a seat on its roof, has been cleaned out and fitted out with bench seating inside. It provides excellent shelter.

Telegraph Bay and Bec du Nez

Jerbourg Point and St Martin's Point together form the bottom right-hand corner of Guernsey. Between them the valley of **Vaux Bêtes** (Valley of the Beasts) runs down to the sea. The bay which is formed by the valley is better known today as **Telegraph Bay**. It was from here that the cable ran under the sea to Jersey. This is a secluded spot frequented more by fishermen than tourists. The strange looking object on the low headland here is a fog signal.

The eastern end of Telegraph Bay makes the headland of **St Martin's Point**. This is not a bold or dramatic headland and there are no shear cliffs here. Instead, there are 300ft slopes which fall gently to sea level. Looking north, you can see all along the coast to Fermain Bay and beyond to the entrance to St Peter Port harbour. It is a view of trees and green gorse covered slopes down to a rocky rim at the water's edge.

Look along the waterline at low water and you'll see a dark line along the rocks marking the high tide level. Just north from here is the ambitiously named **Pine Forest** – in truth little more than a handful of trees – and below you'll find **Marble Bay** named after the marble-like quartz found on the shore there. You can walk to Marble Bay from St Martin's point along a path which follows a low level contour.

Walking further takes you to **Bec du Nez,** an interesting 'out of the way' fishing haven, with good swimming when the tide is not too low. From here you can continue along the cliff path to Fermain if you wish. The entire path between Jerbough and Fermain Bay is in good condition and the distance is reasonable. As you would expect, the views are magnificent, especially in the morning when the sun is rising.

This part of the island offers some interesting 'mix and match' transport options. What about taking the motor launch from St Peter Port to Fermain, then walking to Jerbourg and taking a bus back to St Peter Port.

Return to St Peter Port

Driving back to St Peter Port from St Martin's parish, the main road runs well inland and drops into the town down a busy, long, steep and winding hill which emerges by the former **Guernsey Brewery** and runs towards the **Town Church** and **Harbour**.

If you began your tour of the Island, as the book suggests, in an anti-clockwise direction, setting off northwards from St Peter Port, then now you have come full circle. If you are a cyclist, you'll be thankful that your anti-clockwise tour has enabled you to come down the hill into St Peter Port, rather than requiring you to climb it. If you have just arrived, hired a car and driven in from the airport however, then welcome to St Peter Port, park in the harbour and enjoy the town – there's a great deal to see!

7. Alderney

Imagine you were somehow instantly transported to Sark, Herm, Guernsey, or even Jersey for that matter. How you got there would be a mystery, but it wouldn't take you long to realise you had arrived in the Channel Islands. The granite houses might suggest Brittany, the tiny fields with their banks of earth might encourage you to think of the 'Bocage' region of Normandy, but the sea views at every angle would suggest an island. The warmth and quality of light would then leave you in no doubt as to your general location. A little more in-depth investigation might then reveal which island you had been fortunate enough to land on.

But if your destination had been Alderney rather than any of the other islands, the puzzle would have been more difficult. Alderney is different in almost every respect from the rest of the Archipelago.

Location and culture

Alderney is the second largest island in the Bailiwick of Guernsey. But it is located some 20 miles to the north. From the other islands, you need reasonably good visibility to see it and so, although the Island is only eight miles from the coast of France, there is an

Opposite page: Corblets Bay

Left: Raz Island and Victorian fort linked to Longis Bay by a causeway

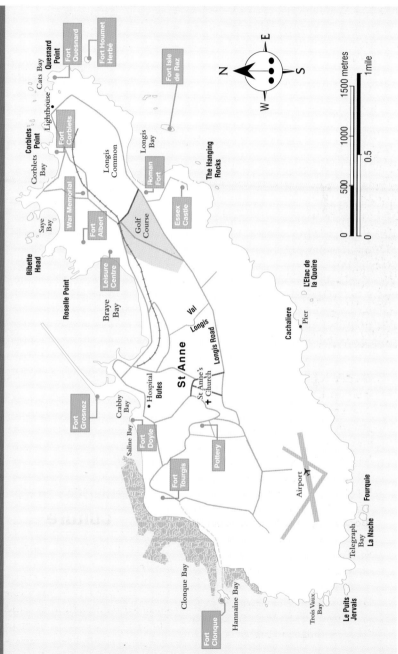

Alderney

Fort Houmet Herbé

Fort Quesnard

Quesnard Point

Cats Bay

Fort Isle de Raz

Lighthouse

Corblets Point

Fort Corblets

Corblets Bay

Longis Bay

Longis Common

Roman Fort

The Hanging Rocks

War Memorial

Saye Bay

Fort Albert

Essex Castle

Bibette Head

Golf Course

Leisure Centre

Roselle Point

L'Etac de la Quoire

Braye Bay

Val

Longis

Cachalière

Pier

Longis Road

St Anne

Hospital

Butes

St Anne's Church

Fort Grosnez

Crabby Bay

Saline Bay

Fort Doyle

Pottery

Fort Tourgis

Airport

Telegraph Bay

La Nache

Fourquie

Clonque Bay

Hannaine Bay

Trois Vaux Bay

Le Puits Jervais

Fort Clonque

N   E   S   W

0   500   1000   1500 metres

0   0.5   1mile

127

air of remoteness here, encouraged by a windswept appearance caused by its inclination to slope eastwards towards France. Alderney's cliffs are in the south and west of the Island and so, in winter, there is no shelter when the cold easterly winds blow in from the Continent.

Measuring 4 miles by 2, Alderney is quite sparsely populated. Only about 2,400 people live here, but there are 13 public houses, which has given rise to the unkind and untrue description of Alderney folk as 'two and a half thousand alcoholics clinging to a rock'. Unlike Guernsey, Alderney's public houses are not restricted on Sundays, the licensing hours are very flexible and they are open seven days per week. Most pubs are open all day.

St. Anne, Alderney's only town, is probably the most French looking town in the Islands, and yet in many respects, the population of Alderney is the most English. St Anne experiences none of the hustle and bustle you would associate with St Peter Port.

There is also a difference in the way in which travellers to the Island are treated. There is little overt commercialisation of tourism so as a visitor you can expect a warm welcome from the community, and then you'll be left in peace while the inhabitants get on with their main activities of fishing, farming, finance, and a little light industry.

In many respects, Alderney has strong similarities with more northerly island communities, Orkney or Shetland for example. Only the weather and the clear sparkling sea suggests that you are in one of Britain's southern islands.

Things to do

Despite its small population and laid-back atmosphere, a surprising amount happens here.

Each **August**, for example, the Island takes on a carnival atmosphere during '**Alderney Week**', a community celebration to which visitors and their families are welcome guests. Festivities begin on the first Monday of the month with a fancy-dress **carnival** with flower-decorated floats, and a local girl as the Island's Queen. In the days following there is an almost endless list of events including crazy attempts at man-powered flights, daft raft races, knock-out cricket, and tug-of-war competitions. At the end of the week there is a spectacular torch-light procession, culminating in a giant bonfire and fireworks display overlooking the harbour. Alderney still celebrates its Bank Holiday at the beginning of August as the UK used to do.

Other events in the annual calendar include a **Juggling Convention,** a **Motor-Racing** hill climb and sprint; an **Open Golf Championship** and an **Angling Festival.** All are well attended by people from all over Europe.

In total, the **Alderney Brochure** lists 42 clubs and societies on the Island, most of which welcome visitors and guests. One which should not be missed is the '**Friends of the Wreck**', an organisation established to support the valuable work being undertaken to recover and preserve the only wreck of an Elizabethan warship ever to be found.

For years the waters around the Island were considered to be a graveyard for shipping and it was well known that there were wrecks of every description beneath the surface. There was great surprise and excitement in 1994 however, when archaeologists found this particular wreck and lifted a complete cannon carriage from the site.

You can learn more about this discovery at the headquarters down by the harbour and see recovered artefacts under preservation. Others may be viewed at the **Museum** which is in the **Old School House**. It is open from Easter to late October and gives a dramatic picture of the Island's past. The collection of archaeology, geology and domestic, marine, and military history from Neolithic times to the present day, is well-displayed. There is also a natural history room.

Like other islands in the archipelago, Alderney has also had its share of **fortress building**. There are 14 Victorian fortresses, and innumerable German bunkers. Unlike the other islands however, most of the Alderney fortifications are accessible to the public. There are also guided specialist tours available although usually a minimum party of 6 is required.

Alderney also has a working pottery which welcomes visitors to see potters at work and demonstrations of spinning and weaving. Refreshments and home-made cakes are also available at the pottery.

Eating out is a good experience in Alderney. The Island has an excellent choice of restaurants, pubs and bistro/cafes, and several have received awards for culinary excellence.

Shopping in Alderney is VAT free and the Island also has its own duty free facilities where visitors (except bailiwick residents) may purchase alcohol and cigarettes at exceptionally low prices from different retail outlets on the Island. Generally shops are open 9.00 am to 5.30 pm Monday to Saturday. Some shops close for lunch and on Wednesday afternoons. A few shops open on Sunday mornings.

Sporting activities

If you like **golf**, Alderney has one of the most scenic courses in the British Isles: a professionally maintained 9-hole course, where the green fees are low and visitors made especially welcome. Clubs are available to hire and you are rarely kept waiting.

For **tennis** fans there are four top-class hard courts and one practice half-court at **Platte Saline.** They cater for everyone, beginners and experienced players alike.

Alderney also has a growing reputation as an ideal base for **fishing holidays**. In summer mackerel, plaice, sole and bass can be caught in large numbers, while in winter, mullet, conger and tope come close inshore. The **Angling Festival** held each October is the highlight of Alderney's fishing calendar. The event attracts anglers from all over Europe and there are big prizes to be won. Seven UK records have been set on the Island.

Sailing is also popular. Alderney is an important port of call for yachts visiting the Channel Islands. Most sailing boat skippers cross the English Channel and head for Cherbourg where they can take stock and check the weather and tides before cruising down into the Channel Islands. They need to do

---

A Tale of the Sea

There is a tale told of a Jersey fisherman who went into one of Alderney's pubs and ridiculed all the local tales of fierce currents and strong tides. Surely they couldn't be any fiercer than the waters around his own native island. Later that day, he took his boat across to the islet of **Burhou** to collect shellfish. When his pannier was full he started back for Braye Harbour.

Two hours later, he has been swept so far southwards that he was in Guernsey waters, but then the tide turned and began to push him northwards again. His fuel soon ran out trying to stem the tide and then he drifted through the Race past Alderney, and almost reached Cherbourg.

On the next ebb, he was seen passing Alderney again as he drifted rapidly down the Swinge back towards Guernsey. Later, the locals found him and towed him back to Braye, where he left his boat and staggered back into the pub. Far gone in thirst and with a new respect for the Alderney fishermen, he silently bought a round of drinks for all!

---

this because the waters surrounding Alderney demand respect. The range of tide here is only half that of Jersey, but the currents can be as much as three times stronger.

Two particularly infamous stretches of water are the **Swinge** and the **Alderney Race**, and you cannot get to the Island without entering at least one of them. There are currents of up to seven knots in both locations. In effect, at times the water can be travelling faster than the top speed of a medium sized sailing boat. Skippers who time their passages to coincide with a favourable current make the trip in super-fast time, others find themselves sailing backwards!

Getting about

Alderney even has its own 'National' airline, **Aurigny,** which offers regular air links with the other Channel Islands and the UK. Blue Island airlines also operates UK and Channel Island air links. So despite its so called remoteness, the Island has a direct and regular air link with the UK through Southampton airport and is in fact, only 12 minutes away from Guernsey by Trislander aircraft.

Arriving by sea is an interesting experience. There are important fishing grounds to the south of the Island and so there is usually plenty of activity to be seen. Look closely at the water and even on a calm day there are patches which appear to bubble and boil. This effect is caused by swift currents travelling across an uneven seabed. At times the water has to rise over rocks, reefs and shoals, and the result is the strangely troubled patches of water which appear turbulent for no visible reason.

The only working **'railway'** in the Channel Islands is located here too. It comprises a two-mile line running from

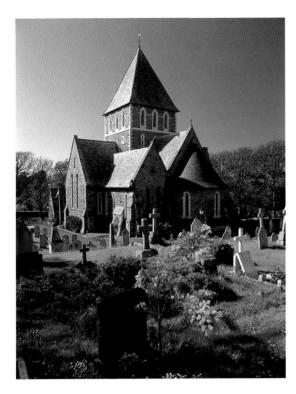

St Annes Church

Christianity

Second century coins have been unearthed in Alderney. Tradition has it that Christianity was brought to the Island by **St Vignalis**. A H Ewan, an authority on the Island's history, disputes this but no matter who the missionary was, it is probable that he arrived here via Brittany. Like other missionaries, he applied the same strategy as in the other islands, and built chapels on or close to sites of ancient religious significance.

Braye Road to **Mannez** on the north-east coast. Originally it was built to transport granite to construct the naval harbour at Braye, but it is now manned by volunteers of the Alderney Railway Society, who provide a regular service at weekends during the summer months. It is a great way to view the Island.

Alternatively, there are excursions by minibus or coach. **Riduna Buses** operate an Island Tour which leaves the taxi rank in **Victoria Street** at 2pm every day. You can book your seat at the Alderney Gift Box (next to the Post Office) or at 'Selections' in Victoria Street.

There are two self-drive **car hire** firms in the Island where you can rent a car, moped or cycle. If you are over seventeen years of age you can hire a moped but you must remember to bring your driving licence. There are two companies which offer bicycle hire.

Although Alderney is the least visited of all the Channel Islands, there is plenty of accommodation available, ranging from hotels which offer nationally recognised standards of service, to unassuming guesthouses. Self-catering accommodation is also available, and there is a campsite where both sites and tents can be hired, but caravans are not allowed on the Island.

By now you should be convinced that at least a day spent in Alderney is worthwhile. Many who undertake the trip, make a point of returning for a much longer stay the following year, and some, like English cricketer **Ian Botham**, grow to love the place so much that they purchase holiday property here.

History

Like Herm and Guernsey, Alderney appears to have been a popular spot with **Neolithic** folk, but much of the evidence for this was destroyed in the nineteenth century by the quarrymen and fortress builders. Today only two Neolithic sites remain: a cist near **Fort Tourgis** on the north west coast, and the remains of an Iron Age site on **Longis Common** in the south east. The cist's ancient name, **Roc à l'Epine**, suggests that a menhir stood here at some time.

Roman remains have also been found on Longis Common. The archaeologist David Johnston suggests that the Roman settlement here was substantial.

The written history of Alderney begins with a **charter** granted by William Duke of Normandy, donating the island to the **Abbey of Mont St Michel** in 1042. Fifteen years later, the island passed into the possession of the Bishop of Coutances where it remained for the following three centuries. Like the rest of the Channel Islands however, its ultimate allegiance was to the English King through his retention of the title '**Duke of Normandy**'.

When Henry VIII came to the throne therefore, he was quick to spot the strategic value of having a 'piece of England' located almost within site of the French port of Cherbourg. Whoever controls Alderney has a great deal of influence over who enters and leaves Cherbourg. With this in mind, he began the process of fortifying the Island and developing the harbour for use as a naval base.

The first harbour was at **Longis**, on the opposite side of the Island to the current harbour at Braye. The remains of the first pier are still visible on the western side of the bay. Work on this pier began in 1546, but came to an end in 1554. The building was not completed until Victorian times.

During the **Civil War**, the Alderney garrison was commanded by Captain Nicholas Ling. He was also the Lieutenant Governor and commander of the Island militia and therefore, when he decided to side with the Parliamentarians, the entire Island did the same. Nicholas Ling retained his power in the island until 1679 when he died at the age of eighty. He built **Government House** in **St Anne's Square**. It is still standing and you can see it today although it is now called the **Island**

Hall, and St Anne's Square has been renamed **Connaught Square**. It is one of the island's finest buildings.

For a while, the Island was governed by the de Carterets from Jersey but then a Guernseyman, Sir Edmond Andros, took over the patent. The **Le Mesurier** family from Guernsey then inherited the Governorship of the Island.

Islander's who preferred a more peaceful and secure form of enterprise traded in cattle. It was fashionable during this period to include one or two Alderneys within English herds. **Alderney Cattle** were a world famous breed long before Jerseys and Guernseys had developed their reputation.

Income from the cattle trade, smuggling and legalised piracy, otherwise known as privateering, paid for the building of a jetty at Braye in 1736 and encouraged the building of warehouses and substantial dwellings close by. The development of Braye as a harbour also encouraged the abandoning of Longis, a harbour which never offered a high degree of shelter.

The new-found Island wealth also paid for substantially better buildings in St Anne. The **Court House** was built in 1770 and **Mouriaux House**, just off **Royal Connaught Square**, built in 1779 is an excellent example of the type of home which successful 'businessmen' would have built.

Coastal fortifications were also improved at this time. In 1811, a **telegraph tower** was built to send visual signals to **Le Mat** in Sark, near the Beauregard Hotel. This made it possible to send signals from Alderney via Sark to Guernsey and Jersey in an instant, enabling the collective fleets and defences of the entire Channel Islands to be alerted within minutes of a French fleet sailing out of Cherbourg.

But consideration was also given to other aspects of life during this period. **John Wesley**, for example, visited the Island in 1789 and, as a result of his visit, a **Methodist Chapel** was built in 1790. It was replaced by a better one in 1814.

Poverty came to Alderney with the ending of the Napoleonic Wars when the Island could no longer depend on income from smuggling and privateering. To make matters worse, the trade in Alderney cattle slumped as the fashion of including Alderneys in UK herds waned. The Island also lost some of its status when General Sir John Le Mesurier surrendered his patent to the crown and became the last hereditary governor of the Island.

Military significance

Despite the ending of hostilities between Britain and France however, the British government continued to regard the French with a high degree of suspicion, particularly in 1842 when the French began to build a massive breakwater and fortifications in **Cherbourg**. From the British point of view, the French actions were a threat to British control of the English Channel. Once again therefore, Alderney, the key to the Channel, became the focus of attention, to monitor the massive engineering works which were being undertaken just a few short miles across the water.

Cruise around Alderney

Throughout this chapter, emphasis has been placed upon the strength of tide, the swiftness of currents, and the occasional turbulence of the seas surrounding Alderney. None of this however, should put you off a boat trip round the Island. Just like the boatmen of Sark and Guernsey, Alderney's small boat skippers are experienced sailors with an encyclopaedic knowledge of the local waters. All the rocks and reefs, and the particular behaviour of the waters at different states of the tide under particular weather conditions, are known to them.

Trips are advertised in Braye Harbour and in St Anne. Chose your trip, step aboard and relax. With a local skipper at the helm, you couldn't possibly be in a safer pair of hands. The particular direction and track of your voyage will depend upon the tide and the strength and direction of the wind.

If your course is to the west, you will pass outside the great **breakwater** and probably head across the **Swinge** towards **Burhou**. Notice the seabirds here, common gulls, oystercatchers, gannets and if you're lucky, puffins. There was a time when they were more numerous, but despite their reduced number, puffins are one of the most charming and popular species to be found. Usually the boat pauses by Burhou to give passengers a chance to study the birds and also to gain a good impression of the rugged shoreline of Burhou.

Further west, **Fort Tourgis** is barely noticeable. It was designed by Captain William Jervios who was careful to soften the harsh military appearance of the fort by making it blend with the landscape. From seaward the success of his endeavour is obvious.

As the boat draws near the **Garden Rocks** (more correctly called Les Etacs), the extent of the colonisation by gannets can be fully appreciated. They arrived and settled here and on Ortac near the Casquetes in the1940s and have since returned each spring.

The breakwater

The British response to the Cherbourg development was to transform the tiny harbour at **Braye** into something entirely different. Although the work was described in official circles as the construction of a 'harbour of refuge', the length and size of the massive breakwater, stretching almost 2,000 yards into the bay, fooled no one. It was plain that the British Government was constructing a port capable of sheltering an entire British fleet if necessary.

In effect, Alderney was to become a **British naval base** only eight miles from the French coast. Today, the break-water is still impressive although only 967 yards are visible, a further 642 yards are submerged beyond the end of the

Boats usually come close in to the base of the cliffs and rocks here. The view is much more powerful from sea level than from cliff tops. All along this coast you'll find crags, caverns, natural arches and green slopes, most of which are invisible from the cliff tops.

As the boat passes **Trois Vaux**, look out for the remains of the small oil tanker *Point Law* wrecked here in 1975. Whenever possible, boats try to enter **Telegraph Bay**. On a lowering trip you may get a glimpse of the beach but the path down to it is barely noticeable. Most passengers however, are amazed by the size of the cave and the enormous rocks here.

Beyond Telegraph Bay, the boat passes the ruins of **Cachalière Pier** and crosses **Bluestone Beach**. Both these places can be reached from landward, although there is always a danger that explorers will be cut off by a rising tide on their return. Once again, the boat trip offers the best and safest view.

Beneath **Essex Castle**, the two **Hanging Rocks** are unmistakable and further on the coast of France will come into view by **Fort Houmet Herbé** – providing the visibility is reasonable. Between here and **Mannez Lighthouse**, the swift flowing currents of the **Swinge** and the **Race** converge, so at times the sea can be quite choppy. Conditions become calmer again after Mannez Lighthouse has been passed. The fort in **Corblets Bay**, now a private house, and **Château à L'Etoc**, now converted into apartments, become visible as you pass by Corblets Bay and into the beautiful **Bay of Saye.**

There are plenty of rocks and gullies to be seen at the base of **Fort Albert** as you sail into **Braye Bay** to complete your circumnavigation of the island. The trip will probably have taken about two hours.

existing pierhead. Had the proposed scheme been carried on to completion, another breakwater of similar size would have been constructed to run out from **Roselle Point** below **Fort Albert**, effectively transforming the entire bay into a harbour of massive proportions.

As well as building the break-water, British Government money was also used to construct a chain of fortifications around the Island at a total cost of £260,000, a great sum in those days, especially in view of the fact that tension between the two powers was easing all through the building programme.

By the time the fortifications were completed they were no longer required. Only **Fort Albert** was regularly used by the military. **Fort Essex** served as

Essex Castle

Essex Castle, which stands on the headland above Longis, was named after the infamous Earl of Essex who, in 1591, bought the governorship of the Island from John Chamberlain who held it from the Crown. It is doubtful whether Essex ever set foot on the island before he in turn leased Alderney to William Chamberlain (John's brother). Shortly afterwards Essex was executed for high treason. Alderney then remained in the hands of the Chamberlain family until 1643, by which time Essex Castle was derelict.

a garrison hospital, and **Fort Tourgis** became a training place for the local militia. **Fort Grosnez** became used by the authorities responsible for the maintenance of the great breakwater.

The building of the breakwater and the coastal defences had a huge impact on the Island. It caused the railway to be built from **Mannez Quarry** to the breakwater and provided employment for hundreds of English workmen, some of whom were housed in specially built accommodation at **Newtown.** It also ensured that British troops were a regular sight within the island. It encouraged better links with the other islands and discouraged close ties with France. Perhaps that is why even today, Alderney 'feels' more English than the other islands in the group.

During the building programme a paddle steamer *The Queen of the Isles* was employed by contractors to bring materials and supplies from Guernsey. Interest in the work was so great however, that she also brought sightseers, the Island's first day-trippers and tourists. This led to the building of **Scott's Hotel** in Braye Road, and other hotels in St Anne. Soon, a regular shipping service

Retaliation

The Germans didn't get everything their own way. Both the RAF and Royal Navy kept close surveillance on activities in the Island and in 1942 a battleship, the *Rodney*, shelled gun emplacements on Alderney from 20 miles away. The German lighthouse keepers on the **Casquets** were taken prisoner by a small commando unit, and also a small raid was carried out on **Burhou.**

Liberation came on the 16th May 1945 when British troops took possession of the Island after the surrender of the German garrison. Unlike liberation in the other Islands where it was an occasion of great joy and relief, the event in Alderney was a sombre occasion. Only a small party of civilians were there to greet the British troops and their main concern was to record stories of German brutality to slaveworkers.

Privateering

John Le Mesurier never gained popularity, but his son Henry seems to have proved more acceptable, probably due to the wealth he brought to the Island through his privateering enterprises. It is recorded for example that in a single year, 1779, his ship *Resolution* earned £134,589 in prize money. By today's standards it is a large sum of money. In those days, it was a vast fortune, and if privateering wasn't to your taste, well there was always a profitable smuggling trade to join. Money was easy, and there was always plenty more to be had providing, of course, that England and France remained hostile to each other.

was established and Alderney gained a reputation, within the Islands at least, as a place of beauty and calm.

War

The First World War had little impact on the Island. Alderney was garrisoned, and troops may have been a little more vigilant during those days but the sight of troops and militia on Alderney was not unusual.

Between the wars, **Alderney Airport** was constructed in 1935. Initially, it was little more than a grass airstrip but it was an improvement on the previous arrangements where aircraft landed and took off from the beach at Braye. Few visitors used the new facilities, however. Air transport was expensive in those days and so the majority of visitors arrived aboard the *Courier*, a steamship which plied between Alderney and Guernsey for many years.

Initially, like the first great conflict, the **Second World War** had little impact upon the Island, but that state of affairs was not destined to last for long. By June 1940, having swept the British into the sea at Dunkirk, the Germans reached Cherbourg and gazed across the narrow passage of water to Alderney. This was

their first view of the British Isles and Alderney must have seemed a glittering prize, ready for the taking.

The populations of Guernsey and Jersey were also worried by the situation and the evacuation of young people, especially school children, had already begun. Both Island authorities kept their populations informed of developments however, and as a result many people elected to stay in the Islands even though they were under threat of invasion.

Evacuation

For some reason however, the 1,400 people living in Alderney were not kept informed of the military situation. They could see the smoke rising from the French coast where retreating troops were setting fire to oil stocks to deny them to the Germans, and they could hear the sound of shell fire. They knew they were the closest to the German threat and so it is not surprising that they became particularly alarmed when the British withdrew their forces in the Island to protect the airfields in Jersey and Guernsey. A few Islanders **evacuated** under their own steam but the majority, feeling isolated and very vulnerable, left en masse under the guidance of Judge J G French.

As a result, when the Germans arrived from Guernsey on 2nd July 1940, there were only seven Islanders remaining in Alderney. In effect, the Island was deserted. Initially, a few Guernsey men were brought to Alderney to assist with farm work and harvesting but their stay was brief and so the Germans had a free hand here. Without a substantial local population, there were no witnesses to report their activities or to temper their excesses.

Compared with their activities in the other Channel Islands, the German occupation of Alderney was the most cruel and barbarous. Hundreds of **slave workers** of every nationality were brought to Alderney to fortify the entire island. They were housed in concentration camps and many died as a result of the inhuman treatment and backbreaking labour.

Under the Germans, all the old forts were strengthened and festooned with barbed wire, the beaches were mined, underwater obstacles were laid, booms were established across some of the bays to prevent landing, a great anti-tank wall was built around Longis Bay, and the entrance to Braye Harbour and the Swinge was guarded by a great gun battery.

Aftermath

Many of the Island's buildings had been destroyed or were in an appalling condition. St Anne's Church had been desecrated and mines, wire and traps lay everywhere. Festivities would have to wait. For a while, the British Government considered abandoning Alderney

for good and leaving it to its fate.

Fortunately, a more positive view prevailed and the decision was taken to reconstruct and rebuild, but it was several months before things were considered safe enough for the Alderney exiles to return to their homes. When they did so, they were appalled at what they saw. Thanks to their determination and substantial aid from Britain and Guernsey, they gradually erased much of the damage which the Germans had inflicted.

Post war developments included a new school, a modernised and extended airport, a hospital, library and museum, improved road surfaces and a significant number of new houses.

Administration

The constitution of the Island was also changed. Unlike other islands, Alderney had never been governed under the feudal system. The traditional form of government had been the '**King's Court**' comprising six jurats, or magistrates and administrators, and a 'Prevot', or Sheriff. In 1949 however, a clear distinction was drawn between the function of the '**Court**' and the '**States**'. The new constitution required a Jurat to chair the Court and a President of the States to preside over the Island Government.

Changes were also made to taxation, education and social services which brought the Island in line with Guernsey and made Alderney much more dependent upon her larger neighbour. In recognition to this, two Alderney deputies attend States of Guernsey meetings.

Places of interest

Braye Harbour

Braye Harbour is on the west coast of the Island, and so no matter from which direction you arrive, the ferry has to enter the **Swinge**. You'll know when you are in it! On a good day, the water looks like a fast flowing river, squeezed between the main coast of Alderney and the tiny island of Burhou. Even without looking, you'll sense the motion. On a bad day, when the breeze is blowing against the direction of the current, the Swinge sets up some short steep waves which race towards the ferry and feel like sold brick walls! It is a constant surprise to visitors, that the roughest part of the journey is the last five or ten minutes, only a few hundred yards from harbour.

Cargo vessels, French fishing boats, visiting yachts, and the occasional warship, berth alongside the **commercial quay** which dates from the start of the present century. The Germans built an extension to this quay during the occupation but in subsequent years it decayed and became dangerous so it was demolished in 1981.

The **Old Jetty** and **Douglas Quay**, beyond the harbour wall at the end of Rue du Braye, form the ancient harbour built in 1763 to accommodate privateers. Boats seldom use these jetties today, largely because of the confined space and the fact that they dry out at low tide. The old granite piers however, provide an ideal shelter and suntrap for visitors.

The breakwater

Braye Harbour is a fascinating place and the great breakwater built by the Victorians is just as impressive from seaward as from the shore. Notice how the wall stands exposed to everything the sea can throw at it. Notice too how the ferry gives the end of the wall a very wide berth to avoid colliding with the submerged section which runs for another 642 yards out into the bay. It is much calmer once you are past the wall inside the bay.

When it was first planned, local seafarers opposed its construction saying that Braye was no place to build a breakwater, as any wall projecting into these notoriously troublesome waters would suffer continual damage from the pounding of heavy seas.

Walk along the Breakwater

Given the right weather a walk along the breakwater can be interesting, but take care because even in summer, the sea can break in spectacular and murderous fashion over the wall for almost its entire length. There are deep recesses built on the harbour side of the breakwater to provide shelter for harbour workers caught in adverse weather. Today they're also used by fishermen and walkers but the best advice, if you have any doubts about the weather, is to stay away from the breakwater and take a stroll somewhere else.

Their advice was accurate although unheeded at the time. Problems were encountered even during the construction of the wall when work was frequently hindered by breaches in the mole caused by stormy weather. The fact that the wall was surplus to requirements even before it was finished, added weight to the constant concern about the high costs of maintenance.

From the Islanders' point of view, the wall was not of their making, they did not ask for a breakwater, they do not own it, and they believed that they could not and should not be expected to find the funds for its upkeep. The accepted compromise has been that Guernsey should bear the largest part of the expense, as its contribution towards the defence of the British Isles. In recent years however, reports and surveys suggest that even this outlay may not be enough and that a further huge investment will be needed to protect the structure against the continual eroding action of the sea. Demolition is one option under consideration although the Islanders almost unanimously oppose the idea.

The fishing harbour

At the landward end of the breakwater, there is a tiny fishermen's harbour, one of the most attractive spots in all the Islands. There are several sheltered places to sit and take in the sights and sounds of a small harbour where the principle activity is still fishing rather than pleasure boating. Here you'll still find the throb of slow-turning diesel engines, the hammering of a repair job, and the clutter of crab-pots, ropes, buoys, and boats in various states of repair.

The **Alderney Sailing Club** and the Harbourmaster's offices are located just above the harbour.

The Railway

Rue du Braye, running from the harbour to the railway station, is a street full of character. On one side, there is a row of eighteenth century houses whose backs are practically on Braye Beach. Two properties, the Sea View Inn and the Diver's Inn, are now public houses. John Wesley stayed at the Diver's Inn during his visit in 1787. On the opposite side of the road, the buildings were constructed as warehouses.

Braye Gates is situated at the landward end of Rue du Braye. Here you'll find Braye Road railway station opened by the **Alderney Railway Society** in 1980. Alderney has the only working rail service in the Channel Islands and Braye Road station is the only ticket office on the line.

Passenger trains run along a length of standard gauge track from here north eastwards to the terminus in **Mannez Quarry** two miles away. Originally built to carry stone from quarries to the harbour for the building of the breakwater, it was opened on 14th July 1847. Queen Victoria and Prince Albert journeyed along the line during their visit to the Island a few years later, in 1854.

Today, a journey along the line from Braye Road takes about fifteen minutes. Having passed the Island school, the route offers interesting views of Braye Bay and the remains of the break-water to which it owes its existence. Later it skirts the golf course and passes **Fort**

Essex. At times, on clear days, the French coast can be seen from the windows.

Passengers have ten minutes to explore Mannez Quarry before the train makes its return journey. In the quarry, on a siding close to the main line, sits a huge self-propelled steam crane – the sole survivor of the 24 originally built in 1944.

Over the years, a number of different engines and rolling stock have been used. Today, the most common sights on the line are the diesel powered railcars *Shirley* and *George*. There are others however. At the beginning of 1981 the **Railway Society** launched a 'steam appeal' and within a year, it was able to purchase a small tank engine called *TJ Daly*. Later, in 1986, a Vulcan Drewry Diesel built in 1949 was given to the Society on loan. This engine called *Elizabeth* is used each weekend when the press of visitors places extra demands on the service. At such times, the Society rolls out its most bizarre acquisition – a pair of bright red 1938 **London Underground** passenger carriages. They were brought to the island in 1987 and have turned the heads of astonished visitors ever since. No matter where you are in the Channel Islands, the nearest tube train is on Alderney. One wonders what will the Railway Society do next? Build the tunnel maybe!

St Anne

Apart from Braye and a cluster of houses at Newtown, St Anne, the Island capital, is the only other centre of population. St Anne is approximately three quarters of a mile from Braye, so it is quite a long uphill walk from the harbour. Buses are available however, and bicycles may be hired at Braye and in town. It is possible to tour the entire island in one day on a mountain bike. If you arrive in the Island by air, St Anne is only a short ten to fifteen minute walk from the airport.

The Butes is a grassy area above the harbour and as good a place as any to begin an exploration of St Anne. Originally, as the name implies, this would have been the Island's archery practice area. It was probably also the training area for the militia. Today however, it is a general purpose sport and recreation area which commands outstanding views across Braye Bay to Burhou, Ortac, Les Casquetes, and much of eastern Alderney. There are extensive sea views. Cricket matches are often played here, and it is doubtful whether there is a more scenic or spectacular cricket pitch to be found anywhere else in the British Isles. At the edge of the green, the former militia gun-sheds are now States workshops. The **Belle Vue Hotel** also adjoins the green.

There is a winding path from the Butes which leads down through gorse and blackberry bushes and rather rough terrain to Braye and the harbour.

Past the **Methodist Church** built in 1852, the Butes adjoin the foot of **Victoria Street**, St Anne's main thoroughfare and named in honour of the visit by Queen Victoria – before then it was known as **Rue Grosnez**. There are shops on both sides of the street but no supermarkets: to walk up Victoria street is to take a step back into an era which predates them. The range of goods may be restricted, but the service and

Alderney has the only working rail service in the Channel Islands

The inner harbour

Braye Harbour breakwater

Cyclist on causeway to Fort Clonque in Alderney

customer care is of a quality belonging to a different age.

St Anne's Church

The **Albert Memorial**, also recalling Alderney's first royal visit, is situated half-way up the street. Through this handsome arch is the main approach to St Anne's Church, a relatively modern church by Channel Island standards, having been designed and built by Sir Giles Gilbert Scott in 1851. The church is located in a hollow, so the tower is not so prominent, but despite this, it is an excellent building in a beautiful setting. The interior is spacious and well proportioned and although it suffered at the hands of the Germans, it has been superbly restored. The modern windows are particularly worth inspecting, especially the window at the east end of the church.

Islander's take special pleasure in hearing the peal of bells, as during the occupation, the Germans removed them and sent them to Cherbourg for melting down. Fortunately, they were recovered from France when the war ended, before this particular act of vandalism could take place.

The Court House

Leaving the churchyard by the south gate brings you to **Queen Elizabeth II Street** and here you will find the Court House built in 1850. The building is used by both the **Court** and the **States**. As with the church, the assembly room has been restored since the German occupation. Today, it contains a valuable painting by John Linnell, which the States acquired in 1981 for £22,000. The picture shows General John Le Mesurier surrendering his patent to the crown, thus ending the line of hereditary governors. The **police station** and gaol adjoin the Court House.

Walking eastwards from here brings you back to Victoria Street a few yards above the **War Memorial Garden**. Close by you'll see the **Post Office** and the Albert Inn. The junction with Ollivier Street is further up Victoria street, and almost opposite there is the **Chez Andre Hotel**. The **Arts Centre** is across the road and further down the street you'll find the **Georgian House Hotel**.

The High Street and Marais Square

The top of Victoria Street runs into the High Street. This used to be the town's main thorough-fare, but now it is secondary to Victoria Street. It is a pleasant street however, which is well worth exploring. Turning left out of Victoria Street takes you along the High Street past the **Jubilee Home for the Elderly** and the **Salvation Army Citadel**.

Le Bourgage is also an interesting old street which runs south from the High Street opposite the Campania public house. The western end of the street leads into **La Venelle de Simon,** a rugged narrow lane which in turn leads to **Le Huret,** near the clock tower. This is a part of St Anne not to be missed. Marais Square, a short way along Le Huret to the left, used to be the site of the great cattle auctions during the period when Alderney cattle were highly prized beasts, considered to be an essential element of any successful English herd. A plaque on the wall of the **Marais Hotel**, and a water trough in the middle of the square, both serve to remind visitors of those days.

On New Year's Day, the Island **Fire Brigade** traditionally turns out for hose-pipe practice in Marais Square, drenching anyone who comes within range!

Royal Connaught Square

A short walk back along Le Huret brings you to Royal Connaught Square, named in 1905 after a visit by the Duke of Connaught. Prior to this date, it had been known as St Anne's Square. Here you'll find the vicarage and the **Royal Connaught Hotel,** but the most impressive building is the **Island Hall,** built in 1763. During its time, it has served as Government House and a convent. These days however, it belongs to the States and is used for dramatic performances, concerts and public meetings, and the Ann French Room has been used for Royal receptions.

The Alderney Library is located in a new building in the grounds of Island Hall

Mouriaux House, just off the square, is one of most stately residences and probably the best private dwelling in the Island. Unfortunately, it faces a rather ugly tower built by the Germans.

The Museum

No visit to St Anne can be complete however, without a visit to the **Alderney Society's** Museum which is not far from here. Close by, an ancient clock tower and graveyard are all that remains of the old parish church which once stood on this spot.

The museum, once the Island school, was extensively renovated, extended and opened by the Queen Mother in May 1984. It is divided into twelve sections, each of which concentrates upon a different aspect of Island history. There are **Stone** and **Bronze Age** artefacts including a 4,000 year old spear, and numerous Roman objects taken from the **Nunnery** site. There are also many relics from the German occupation, nautical exhibits, and pictures and photographs illustrating the history of fishing, farming and other aspects of Island life. An inscription over the door dates the building at 1790.

Ollivier Street, Le Val and Les Rocquettes

To complete an exploration of the town, return from the museum eastwards along the High Street until you reach the Coronation Pub at the top of Victoria Street, retrace your steps back down Victoria Street until you reach Ollivier Street and then follow this street until you arrive at **Le Val,** a road which runs from Braye Harbour to the High Street. For Islanders, Le Val is something of a town by-pass.

You can walk down Le Val past the Island dairy, to Les Rocquettes by the Roman Catholic Church of **St Ann and St Mary Magdalen,** which was built in 1958. Continue on down Le Val, if you are heading for the harbour or railway station. Alternatively, follow Les Rocquettes to arrive back at the bottom of Victoria Street. A steep cobbled lane runs down from here to **The Terrace,** a pleasantly wooded public garden. From the Terrace, a very attractive road, **The Valley**, leads down to **Saline Bay** and **Crabby.** This too takes you back towards the harbour.

The rest of Alderney

Although Alderney has a reputation for it's high 'pub to population' ratio, most of these are located in St Anne or Braye and there are few other places on the Island to obtain refreshments. Once you travel further afield, it's important that you take whatever refreshments you may need with you.

Having issued that warning, it has to be said that Alderney is a delightful place to explore on foot, bicycle, by train or as part of an organised coach tour. On a mountain bike you can circumnavigate the entire Island in a day. Generally speaking the roads are good, and many of the paths are wide. A mountain bike will get you to and from most places.

The east side

Eastwards from **Braye**, there is easy travelling along the sands, by road or across the grass. No matter how you travel, the sea views are always interesting. **Fort Albert** on **Mount Touraille** was the master fort of the Island. Today however, it is derelict and closed to the public. Beneath the fort is the **Mount Hale Battery,** the arsenal and the former garrison football pitch.

There is a rough road from **Whitegates House** at the crossroads to the fort's gates. It then continues around to a point overlooking Braye Harbour. Just below is **Roselle Battery** where a Second World War searchlight battery used to be located. This area was one of the most heavily fortified during the occupation and there is still plenty of evidence around today.

During the nineteenth century, when the British had a garrison here, Fort Albert would have been in immaculate condition. Today however, there is an air of desolation and ruin. The States of Alderney are the current owners of the fort, but no decision has been taken about its future.

Beyond Fort Albert the road forks at the **Hammond Memorial**, a simple yet poignant reminder of the slaveworkers of all nationalities who died in the Island during the occupation. The left hand fork takes you to **Fort Château à l'Etoc** on the eastern side of **Saye Bay**. The **Hermitage Battery** is just behind, standing near the site of the original Château. The present château is a Victorian structure with a little bit of 'German occupation' thrown in for good measure.

Before arriving at the château however, there is a turning on the left just after the fork. This leads to **Saye Bay**, **Bibette Head** and the islet of **Houmet des Pies**. This beautiful part of the Island was the spot where garrison troops used to bathe. The beach is clean and the sands are inviting. There are sand dunes on the landward side close to **Saye Farm**, the Island's official camp site**.**

The eastern shore of **Château à l'Etoc** is called **Arch Bay**, so named because of a tunnel under the road leading to the fort. In times gone by, it was used by farmers collecting Vraic (seaweed) from the beach for use as fertiliser on the fields.

Mannez

Opposite Fort Corblets are quarries, the largest of which is **Mannez Quarry**

Braye Bay and Fort Albert

just along the road where the railway terminus and the engine sheds are located. High above the quarry stands a most obvious relic of the German occupation, a massive concrete **observation tower**. All around its entrance above the quarry there are remains of other German defence works, which suggest that this was an important military location. Viewed from the entrance it is quite an imposing structure, but to gain a real feeling for its size, weight, and power, stand in the quarry and look up at it towering over you. It is an impressive sight.

Mannez Lighthouse is a short walk from the quarry. It is open to visitors most afternoons and the view from its lantern is vast; at night, the beams can be seem from many locations within the Island. By the side of the lighthouse stands the **foghorn**, responsible for making one of the saddest and most depressing sounds known to mankind.

Seaward from the lighthouse stands **Fort Les Homeaux Florains**. It can only be reached after a rock climb and a short swim. The place is in ruins, so the effort hardly seems worth it,

especially as **Fort Quesnard** is just a short walk beyond.

Longis

From the lighthouse, the main road turns inland and doesn't return to the sea until it reaches **Longis Bay**. There is however, a coastal path from Fort Quesnard to the bay, which has the reputation of being one of the best walks in the Island. The coastline here is wild and rocky and full of interest. The ruins of **Fort Houmet Herbé** stand atop an islet in **St Esquere Bay**

Manez lighthouse

147

A short walk

After a day of touring, golf or fishing here, there is a delightful short walk which you could undertake from St Anne for an evening stroll before dinner or perhaps for a picnic. Begin in **Connaught Square** and walk past **Les Mouriaux House** onto a field track which runs westwards past modern houses. The track crosses **Little Blaye** and for a while it becomes indistinct. Carry on westwards however towards a copse which conceals a path leading to an embankment known as **Martin's Bridge** which crosses a shallow valley. A stream runs from here to **Watermill Farm** below **Fort Tourgis**. By the side of the embankment there is a beautiful garden. Across the embankment the path takes you to the main road. It is only a short walk from here to the airport and back to St Anne.

and are accessible at low tide. Various gullies along the way are good for bathing when tidal conditions permit.

Longis Bay is a favourite spot for visitors. Its sands are broad and fine and the great German anti-tank wall provides excellent shelter from the wind. Just offshore, joined by a causeway to the beach, stands **Fort Islet de Raz**. It is accessible at all times except high water and is well worth a visit, even if only to stand on the battlements and gain a new view of the Island. In addition however, the fort houses a collection of stuffed birds and an art gallery.

The Nunnery, site of an old **Roman fort**, is at the other end of Longis Bay. It never was a real nunnery, but according to legend it earned its name because the garrison there found it so lonely. Today, although it is a private residence, some of the ancient walls are still there to be seen, although others have collapsed and now lie on the beach. Close by the Nunnery there is **The Barn Restaurant**, a rare out-of-town location for food and refreshments.

Longis Common lies inland from the Nunnery. Today it is a fairly desolate place with only a few dwellings, some evidence of quarrying and German defence works, but in Neolithic times it was probably a more popular spot. This is where most of the **Neolithic remains** were found during the nineteenth century. Sadly, the majority of sites were destroyed.

One important piece of prehistory survives however, an **Iron Age** site which was discovered in 1968 during the laying out of the golf course. There is a sign to indicate the way to it a few yards along the road opposite the Nunnery. It is believed that the site was once a workshop where pottery was made. There is not much to see there now, but the objects found can be viewed at the museum. Across the road, at **The Kennels**, the remains of a supposed Roman building were unearthed.

There are several ways back to St Anne from the Nunnery. The **Rue des Mielles** crosses the Island and takes you back to Whitegates near Fort Albert, or the **Route des Carieres** takes you westward into Route de Longis which eventually becomes St Anne's High Street.

Alternatively there is a cliff path which takes you up past Essex Castle before bringing you out on Route de Longis, or you can use **Essex Glen** via an inconspicuous entrance opposite the Barn Restaurant. This route can occasionally be damp underfoot, but it is an interesting walk which brings you to the Longis road near **Devereux House Hotel**. St Anne is then a short walk westwards.

The west side

Westward from Braye there is a good road past the power station and along the shores of **Crabby Bay** and into

Hanging Rocks

Essex Castle, restored in Victorian times and used for a while as the old garrison hospital, stands on imposing cliffs with German fortifications all around. Below them, halfway down the slopes, are the **Hanging Rocks** – a pair of great rocks which lean over like the Tower of Pisa.

Legend has it that a boatfull of visiting Jerseymen attempted to acquire Alderney by lashing a rope around these rocks and endeavouring to tow the island away. They managed to tilt the rocks but achieved nothing else!

By Essex Castle the path widens out and becomes a road, offering views of Longis Bay and the eastern end of the island as it skirts the castle walls and drops down towards the **Nunnery.**

Saline Bay. This is the shore of the infamous **Swinge**, a place of high seas and strong currents, so it is not the best location in the Island for swimming. Heavy seas frequently pound the shore here and, even on a good day, you would need to be a strong swimmer. **Fort Platte Saline,** in the middle of the bay, is hardly recognisable as a fort. It is owned and used by a company which excavates and exports sand from the beach.

At the western end of Saline Bay, **Petit Val Road** leads inland and rises along the side of **Fort Tourgis,** but the coast road continues further along the shore underneath the outer walls of the fort, past innumerable defence works of Victorian and twentieth century vintage, towards **Fort Clonque.**

By the entrance to Fort Tourgis towards the summit of Petit Val Road, stands the **Tourgis Dolmen.** It isn't much to look at by Channel Island standards, but Fort Tourgis on the other hand is well worth inspecting, from the outside at least. A sign at the entrance warns visitors not to enter. Be very careful if you choose to ignore the sign. It is a derelict building, the brickwork and plaster are unsound and its floors are rotten and unsafe. There is a track from the Fort which runs down to meet the coast road at **Clonque Cottage.** The beach here is rocky, ideal for explorers who enjoy rock pools.

To seaward there is **Burhou**, and further offshore **Ortac,** unmistakable with its white peak, and in the distance the lighthouse on the lonely **Casquets** stands as a permanent reminder of the dangerous navigation in these waters.

Aurigny: Alderney's 'National' Airline

Alderney people are proud of their own airline which, over the years, has become a symbol of the independence of the Channel Islands. The distinctive yellow aircraft are affectionately known to Islanders as 'the yellow perils', but they have also gained an international reputation thanks to the series of children's books, the *Little Yellow Plane Adventures* written by Peter Seabourne, which feature **Joey**, a plane character based on one of Aurigny's Trislander aircraft which has the registration G-JOEY.

Trislanders are the main aircraft used on inter-island routes and until recently they were all painted bright yellow. Currently there are seven in service. Today, one or two have been repainted in the livery of prestigious Island companies. Despite the colour changes, however, their three engine configuration and 'boxy' shape make them highly distinctive aircraft.

Trislanders accommodate 17 people and have a cruising speed of 267 km/h at 8,000 ft, but Aurigny aircraft rarely reach this height. Between the Islands they fly at 1,000 or 2,000 feet depending on the destination. From Jersey to Guernsey, for example, they fly at 1,000 ft. From Guernsey to Jersey however, they fly at 2,000 ft in order to ensure a safe vertical distance between aircraft. At such heights, the views are outstanding.

Aurigny also operate flights to and from **Southampton,** and on this route, the company frequently uses a Short 360. This is powered by two Pratt and Whitney turboprop engines. It has a maximum speed of 393 km/h at 10,000 ft, but once again, Auringny craft rarely operate at this height. En-route from Guernsey to Southampton for example, you are more likely to travel at 8,000ft. The Short can carry 36 passengers.

The service which Auringy operate is as much like a bus service as an airline between Guernsey and Jersey. For example, the planes operate a half hour schedule and everything is done to keep administration to a minimum. To this end, the company operates from its own premises, wherever possible taking care of its own ticketing, baggage handling and boarding.

When you fly Aurigny therefore, don't be surprised to find that the person who checks your ticket is also the person who takes you to the plane, loads your baggage and helps you aboard. The friendly and informal approach to inter-Island airtravel which Aurigny offers, can create a feeling that you are taking a step back in time. Perhaps this is flying like it used to be.

Once inside the Trislander, that feeling is reinforced by the fact that you are sitting within a few feet of the pilot, who usually turns round and talks to you over his shoulder about safety precautions and seatbelts! Passengers located near the front of the aircraft will even be able to see the instrument panel and read the dials. For those who cannot, the in-flight magazine usually contains a page which details all the controls and explains what they do.

Don't let this put you off. All new pilots starting with Aurigny are highly experienced, many having begun their careers with the RAF or large commercial airlines. They are put through intensive initial training to ensure that they are completely familiar with the company's aircraft, and they undertake six monthly training sessions to test their ability to handle every kind of emergency situation which could occur. They are subject, too, to a medical examination every six months!

With flight times of only 15 minutes between Guernsey and Jersey and only 12 minutes between Guernsey and Alderney, a trip on one of the Joey's can be the highlight of any Channel Island holiday.

Corblets Bay

From Chateau a l'Etoc, there is a road which runs along Arch Bay and Corblets Bay eastwards to join the main road at **Fort Corblets**. Many people argue that Corblets Bay is the best in the Island. The sands are clean and fine, the swimming is safe, and the surf is usually good. The rocks are interesting to examine but hard to sit on because the strata is uptilted. There is a bus stop here.

The road runs around the gardens of Fort Corblets, an elegant residence, with little remaining evidence of German handiwork.

Burhou Island

This island is about a half mile in length and 250ft (76m) wide. By Channel Island standards she is fairly low lying, with the highest point standing only about 40ft above sea level.

Before the last war, a French couple lived and farmed on the Island but their cottage was destroyed by German gunners during the occupation who used it for target practice. Today the small cottage has been rebuilt and nearby a wildlife observation hide has been set up. Despite this, the rugged rock formations and the scant vegetation give the impression of a wild and desolate place.

Burhou is home to a large population of rabbits and some puffins but there is no fresh water, so anyone wishing to stay overnight on the Island will need to take all their own provisions. Permission must also be obtained from the **States Offices** in **Queen Elizabeth II Street**.

On the western side of Burhou stands **Little Burhou,** separated at high tide by a racing torrent of water. Beyond Little Burhou there is a large reef and further on another known as **Le Renonquet** – the final resting place of the *Viper,* a Royal Navy vessel which was stranded here during thick fog in 1901. Botanists take great interest in Burhou and her smaller sister. Despite their proximity, the vegetation on each island is completely different.

The great **Ortac Stack** stands 79ft (24m) out of the sea between Burhou and Les Casquets. It is rarely visited, although it may be possible to arrange to be dropped off and collected from there by a local boatman if you wish. Since 1940, Ortac has been home to a large colony of gannet. It is easy to climb and the birds are said to tolerate human visitors, but be careful.

Back on the mainland

Fort Clonque, owned and maintained by the Landmark Trust, has been converted into holiday apartments. It lies offshore at the end of Clonque Bay. You can reach it by walking along the causeway at anytime except high tide.

Hannaine Bay is next, a sheltered spot with good bathing when its sands are exposed. There are no paths further along the coastline after Hannaine Bay. From here, the way winds and zig-zags uphill towards an area of the Island known at **La Giffoine**.

Alderney has few signposts and with a twisting and turning path, it is easy to become confused here. Generally speaking, the path takes you through the fields until you arrive at a road which runs towards the south west (away from St Anne). The second turning on the right off this road, takes you along a rough path leading to the **Heights of La Giffoine.** There used to be a beacon here, but the massive German defence works replaced it.

Below the defences, a path leads some way down the cliff to offer a view of the **Garden Rock** and its colony of gannets. **Trois Vaux Bay** lies just beyond. As the name suggests, three valleys converge at the cliff edge here. There is no obvious path down to the water so access to the bay is difficult. Most visitors are happy to gaze at view from the cliff tops and then return to the road by **Le Clos des Cables.**

Les Casquets

Situated nine miles from Alderney, this feels like one of the loneliest places on earth. Some form of beacon has stood here since 1785 when a coal fire was burned to warn shipping of the dangers. The present lighthouse contains a lantern of 2,850,000 candle power, which is visible from 17 miles away. *HMS Victory*, the fourth Royal Navy vessel to carry the name, sank here in 1744 with the loss of over 1,000 crew.

Later in 1899, this was the scene of an equally harrowing disaster when the *Stella*, the Channel Island ferry and mailboat, struck the rocks at top speed in thick fog while attempting to beat a rival. 102 people lost their lives on that occasion.

Telegraph Bay

There is no precise footpath along the clifftops between **Trois Vaux** and **Telegraph Bay** but a right turn from the road takes you southwards along the end of the airport runway. Another right turn then leads you down towards the steps which run into Telegraph Bay. The views from the clifftops are excellent, but to really comprehend the size of the cliffs and the height of both **La Nache** and **La Fourquie**, a pair of tremendous rocks standing out of the bay, you need to climb down to the beach. It is an easy descent, although the climb back can be hard going. There are caves and rock pools here and the bathing is excellent. On most occasions you'll have the place to yourself, but pay particular attention to the state of the tide. On a rising tide, the base of the cliff path can become cut off from the beach. Take care.

You can return to the road via another path running from the eastern end of the bay. This takes you past **Telegraph Tower**, a German construction which is now closed to the public. Eastward from here the road flanks the airport, staying well away from the coast. There are occasional paths running to the cliff tops from the road, but generally they are ill-defined.

At the eastern end of the airport the road turns inland towards St Anne, but you can continue along the coast by following the cliff path from here. Anglers and naturalists use this path to visit the ruined pier at **La Cachalière** or to scramble to **Bluestone Bay**. As with Telegraph Bay though, access to and from these areas is dependent upon the state of tide. Take care not to be stranded.

All along the cliff path here, there are tracks which lead back inland to St Anne so it is possible to cover as much or as little of the cliff path as you wish. If you decide to stay with the path as far as **La Haze**, you will be rewarded with the sight of the Island's rubbish tip. Well they had to put it somewhere!

8 Sark, Herm & Jethou

SARK

Eight miles east of Guernsey, the beautiful island of Sark towers 200ft out of the sea. It is, in fact, almost two islands, joined by a narrow 'bridge' of land a mere 10 metres wide. All in all, Sark is just three and a half miles in length and one and a halfmiles wide. The 1991 census revealed a population of 650.

Sark & Herm

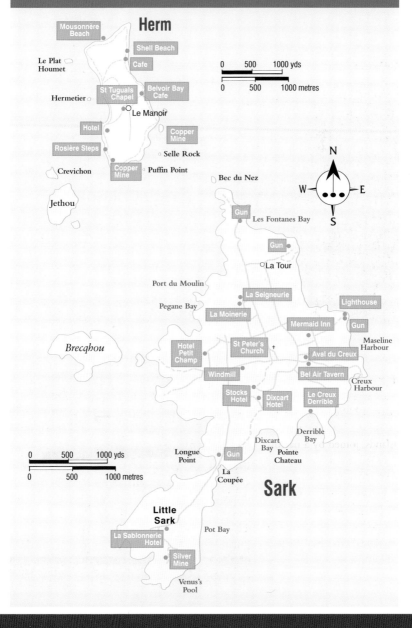

Herm

Mousonnère Beach

Le Plat Houmet

Shell Beach

Cafe

St Tuguals Chapel

Belvoir Bay Cafe

Hermetier

Le Manoir

Hotel

Copper Mine

Rosière Steps

Selle Rock

Crevichon

Copper Mine

Puffin Point

Jethou

Bec du Nez

0   500   1000 yds

0   500   1000 metres

Gun

Les Fontanes Bay

Gun

La Tour

N
W   E
S

Port du Moulin

La Seigneurie

Lighthouse

Pegane Bay

La Moinerie

Mermaid Inn

Gun

Brecqhou

Hotel Petit Champ

St Peter's Church

Aval du Creux

Maseline Harbour

Windmill

Bel Air Tavern

Creux Harbour

Stocks Hotel

Dixcart Hotel

Le Creux Derrible

Derrible Bay

Dixcart Bay

Longue Point

Gun

Pointe Chateau

La Coupée

Sark

0   500   1000 yds

0   500   1000 metres

Little Sark

Pot Bay

La Sablonnerie Hotel

Silver Mine

Venus's Pool

Of all the Channel Islands, Sark is probably the one which is regarded with the greatest affection. For most of us, this is the community which we would love to join. These are the people who turned their backs on the twentieth century and profited by doing so. The fact that Sark has no motor vehicles other than farm tractors, has its own 'feudal parliament', and doesn't allow aeroplanes to fly over the Island let alone land there, has become so embedded in the public imagination, that a sense of romance and fantasy colours most peoples' views of the Island.

Unlike most other places though, the further you delve into the history and reality of life on Sark, the more fantastic the picture becomes.

History

To understand Sark you must begin with its history. Unlike the other Channel Islands, Neolithic remains on Sark are relatively few. Perhaps those two hundred foot cliffs towering out of the rock strewn sea discouraged early settlement. Perhaps the difficulty of landing on Sark and the ease of landing on nearby Herm helps to explain the few remains on Sark and the disproportionately large number of Neolithic sites just across the water.

Despite the difficulties of landing however, tradition has it that **St Magloire,** a cousin of St Sampson, brought Christianity to the Island when he visited Sark in the middle of the sixth century. It is said that he came with a group of sixty monks who established an oratory and cells on the present site of the **Seigneurie**. Nearby there is an old house called **La Moinerie,** which could have been St Magloire's monastery.

From then until about 1550 the history of Sark is complicated and, at times, somewhat vague. Standing between the two great but fractious nations of France and England, it was inevitable that Sark's history would not have been peaceful. It is clear that at times the Island was occupied and fortified by the French, but at other times it appears to have been in no-man's land, in the temporary ownership of whoever scaled the cliffs. Occasionally Sark was used as a pirate stronghold, being well-placed to attack Channel shipping.

First settlement

It was probably the uncertain status of Sark and the constant threat of occupation by hostile forces which prompted a Jerseyman, **Helier de Carteret**, Seigneur of the Fief de St Ouen (Lord of the manor of St Ouen) to petition Queen Elizabeth I for permission to colonise the island and establish a settled community there. Having gained the necessary permission in "Letters Patent", Helier, his wife Margaret and a number of their St Ouen tenants, moved to Sark in 1565 and began a settlement, bringing everything they needed with them.

In order to ensure that the Island would never again become depopulated, he parcelled out blocks of land at a low rental, large enough to support a family, on condition that a house was put up and the tenant provided one man, armed with a musket and ammunition, to defend the Island if necessary.

One sixth of Sark he retained for

himself, and on it he built his house, **Le Manoir**. **Beauregard**, the second largest site on the island went to the **Gosselin** family of Guernsey, on condition they provided four men and paid a rent set at 50 shillings. Other parcels comprising pieces of farmland and portions of cliff grazing known as a **'cotil'** went to those who had accompanied Helier. Various other members of the de Carteret family made up many of the remaining numbers.

Helier de Carteret's scheme was hugely successful and within a short space of time, the neglected land was brought under cultivation, houses were built, roads were laid and a harbour was constructed. By 1572 the settlement was established and Helier travelled to England to present the Queen with his report. Elizabeth made Sark a separate Fiefdom from St Ouen and gave it to Helier and his heirs in perpetuity. Helier therefore became the first **Seigneur**.

Administration

As you would expect of a man who had himself been a beneficiary of the feudal system in Jersey, Helier imposed a feudal form of government on Sark. The laws which he devised were constructed with the aim of maintaining a cohesive community based upon the original forty parcels of land. The system works like this:— each of the forty leaseholders or tenants has an automatic membership of the **Chief Pleas** — Sark's feudal parliament. To maintain the correct number of members sitting in the Chief Pleas, leases cannot be split or divided. A man's eldest son is his heir and, for this reason, **divorce is not allowed** in the island. If divorce

were to be allowed, sons from different marriages could contest tenancy of their late father's land and this would create a serious constitutional crisis for the community.

Today, although a few changes and developments have taken place, Helier de Carteret's feudal system is still alive and well in Sark. In many respects the Island is still run the way it was 433 years ago. The Seigneur still presides over the Chief Pleas, which comprises the forty tenants, although now they are joined by twelve deputies who are elected by the population of 650. Some Crown-appointed officers make up the administration — a 'Seneschal' or judge, a 'Greffier' or registrar, and a 'Prevot' or Sheriff. Although Sark is a part of the Bailiwick of Guernsey, in most respects the Island looks after its own affairs, and it seems to do well without cars, income tax, and much of the legislation passed by the European Union.

When he considered it safe to do so, Helier de Careret returned to Jersey, leaving his son Phillipe as the second Seigneur. Since then there have been twenty one seigneurs, three of whom were women known as **'Dames'**. The most well-known was probably Dame Sybil Hathaway, famed for summoning the invading Germans to her home and then keeping them waiting until she was ready to meet them. Dame Sybil was the grandmother of Mr Michael Beaumont, the present Seigneur. As you would expect, he has certain rights and privileges which he does not share with the local population, for example, as the Seigneur he is the only Island resident allowed to own pigeons or an unspayed bitch!

Images of Sark

Sarks' dramatic west coast

La Grande Grêve

War

Since the adoption of feudal law and order, the Island's history, save for the German occupation,has been largely uneventful. In the Napoleonic wars, guns were mounted on Sark's headlands, and today they're still there – rusty and neglected, but still pointing towards France. The Sark militia, formed from the male population of the Islandaccording to the terms of their feudal leases, remained active until 1880. It was then stood down, and one of the brass fieldguns was melted down and recast as the church bell. More than one person has drawn attention to the 'guns to ploughshares' analogy.

Other relics of the days of the militia include cannon, to be found in the grounds of Le Seigneurie, a ruined militia guardhouse at L'Eperquerie, the remains of the shooting butts and the Arsenal, to be found close-by the tiny Island prison.

During the Second World War, Sark was occupied by the Germans, but it is generally felt that the community herewas dealt with lightly in comparison to experiences in the other islands. Some Islanders were deported and there were restrictions, but food was more plentiful than on the other islands, and the frenetic activity of building fortifications which took place elsewhere, did not happen here.

The economy

During the nineteenth century, **Little Sark** was the location of a great deal of futile mining activity. The **Le Pelley** family, which took over the lordship of theIsland from the de Carteret's, employed 250 Cornish miners to dig four mineshafts on Little Sark. They were looking for silver, copper, and lead, but despite an investment of over £30,000, they gained nothing from it. In the end, saddled with debt, the family was obliged to transfer the Seigneurie to Mrs T G Collings. The present Seigneur is of Collings descent.

Tourism

Strangely enough, although the mines failed, they proved tobe instrumental in developing tourism in the Island, which has provided an excellent source of income for the community.

The mine workings attracted a number of visitors from Guernsey who, having seen the mines,began to explore the rest of the Island and became enchanted by the beauty of what they saw.Word quickly spread and theadvent of reliable steam vessels in the 1850s encouraged day trip visitors from the other islands.

This led to the rapid development of an Island tourist infrastructure to cater for increasing numbers of visitors, some of whom wished to make more prolonged visits. Hotels were built, the harbour was improved and carriages were bought to provide transport for tourists. Gradually, farming and fishing, the mainstays of Island economy, were overtaken in importance by tourism.

The Sark Lark

Since the war, Sark's economy has developed even further and its fame as a tourist location has spread world wide but more recently in the 1990s the Island gained international fame if not notoriety, for its development as a haven for companies wishing to avoid payment of taxes.

According to the *Daily Telegraph,* there were 23,000 companies registered in the Island – about forty per head of population. This practice known as the 'Sark Lark' created concern and condemnation world wide. It was alleged that some Islanders earned up to £100,000 per year by running 'offshore bases', described by some writers as nothing more than outhouses and sheds crammed with fax machines and telephone lines. One resident was alleged to have 2,300 directorships.

Times have changed, however, and today as visitor to the Island, you'll find no evidence of the finance industry, shady or otherwise, as you explore the paths and lanes of this unique community. In fact, given the pressures for growth and expansion created by tourism and finance, it is surprising how well people here have managed to maintain the traditional way of life and preserve the outstanding natural beauty of the Island.

Getting there

The only way to arrive in Sark is by sea. **The Isle of Sark Shipping Company** runs regular passenger and cargo services to the Island and the trip generally takes about forty minutes. As with any sea voyage in these waters, navigation is generally done by lining up landmarks to keep the vessel in the deep water passages. There are several twists and turns on the route which add interest to the voyage and bring the vessel close in to several coasts on the way.

On the outward passage, you'll run in very close along the southern shore of **Jethou**, and if you can take your eyes off its beauty for a while, you'll notice some needle sharp rocks to seaward too. Passing Jethou, you are then given an excellent view of the southern coast of **Herm,** and as the distance increases, the view widens to include **Shell Beach** and the entire eastern shore.

Usually, the ferry runs around the northern tip of Sark before starting the final leg of its journey to Maseline Harbour. The deep water passage brings the craft close inshore here, and at times it seems as if you could reach overboard and touch the Island. The currents are strong at this point of the passage, and given the right state of tide, you'll notice that the water seems to be running almost like a river, so you can expect the vessel to roll somewhat even on the calmest day.

It is from here that the full impact of the grandeur of the cliffs can be appreciated. It is also remarkable that there are very few buildings to be seen as you pass down the east coast. Only the lighthouse at **Point Robert** is really conspicuous, but even this structure is located half-way down the cliff face so it doesn't dominate or detract from the wild scene. The Island is a high plateau so, from the deck of the ferry, most of the human activity is taking place between 200 and 320 ft above you.

Maseline Harbour was constructed in concrete and was officially opened by HRH the Duke of Edinburgh on the occasion of the Queen's visit to the island in 1949. She was the first monarch to set foot in the Island. Maseline is tiny but it offers deepwater access at all states of the tide, unlike the island's original harbour at nearby Creux, which dries out at low water.

Getting about

Passengers disembark on the tiny quay and then walk through a tunnel in the cliff face to emerge at the bottom of a steep hill leading to the top of the plateau and the interior of the Island. The road is unmetalled, steep and dusty. If you insist on walking, there is a footpath on the left hand side which leads up through the wooded valley side, avoiding the road yet arriving at the same spot at the top of the hill. Most visitors however, choose to save their energy and travel up the hill by '**toast-rack**', a local term used to describe one or two fairly rudimentary tractor-drawn buses which carry passengers to the top for about 50 pence. If you wish to travel up the hill in grander style, you can hire the services of a horse-carriage and driver, but you'll need to book this in advance.

The toast-racks stop almost at the top of the hill by the **Aval du Creux Hotel** and the **Bel Air Pub**. Both are popular spots. There is some self-catering accommodation close-by and usually there are carriages here waiting to take visitors around the Island. The majority are four wheeled wagons, but there are lighter two-wheeled traps also. The horses are strong, docile, amiable creatures, descended from animals which probably used to pull the ploughs.

By carriage

A carriage tour of the Island is a delightful way to spend a couple of hours, especially if there is a true Sarkee in the driving seat. They know the Island best and naturally give the best commentaries. Occasionally, when two carts meet, you may here a snippet of **Sark-French**, the old language, which, as you would expect given Sark's history, is much closer in origin to Jersey-French than Guernsey-French.

The carriages have a number of set routes, although the most usual tour takes you out towards **L'Eperquerie**, the original landing place of the settlers in 1564. It remained in use as the harbour until **Creux** was built.

The trip takes in views of Brecqhou, Herm, Jethou, and Guernsey. On Mondays and Wednesdays, most tours take you to the grounds of the **Seigneurie** and give you time to visit the gardens there, before returning you to the top of Harbour Hill. If you'd prefer not to make the full island tour by carriage, you can use them like taxis.

By cycle

Hiring a bicycle is a cheap and popular alternative to the carriage tour. They can be hired near where the tractor-drawn buses stop at the top of **Harbour Hill**, or further along **The Avenue.** Given the absence of motor vehicles other than tractors, and the gentle nature of the terrain, cycles are an ideal means of transport on Sark. With a cycle, you can explore the entire Island in a day.

Centre of Sark

Continuing up the hill, by cycle, on foot or by carriage, brings you to **La Collinette** crossroads, an important spot from which to take your bearings. The village is just beyond. There is a modern pottery here, a cycle hireshop

There are no cars on Sark. Horse and carriage, tractors and bikes are used for getting around

and, down **Rue Lucas**, the **Mermaid Tavern** caters well for thirsty travellers.

The main part of the village however, is further on, strungout along the main road known as the Avenue. It is a rather ramshackle collection of buildings comprising a couple of general stores, gift shops, banks andprivate dwellings.

Beyond the village shops the Avenue forks. The right fork leads down a road built in 1820 at the cost of £1,000, to **St Peter's Church,** built in the same year. Although the church itself is not remarkable, it is well cared for and has a simple dignity, appropriate to the Island community. The clock tower is conspicuous and provides an ideal landmark.

The small stone built school next door, also acts as Sark's **House of Parliament.** This is where the **Chief Pleas** holds its quarterly meeting, and where the court sits when necessary. Children get a school holiday whenever either body meets during school term-time.

If you continue along this road to its end, you'll arriveat L'Eperquerie, Helier de Carteret's original landing place in 1564.

The left fork at the end of the Avenue lead to the **Manoir**, once the home of the Seigneur. Opposite is a junior school and a tiny two-celled prison, mainly used to accommodate those who have enjoyed too much of the duty free drink during their visit to the island. More serious criminals are sent to Guernsey for trial and punishment.

Further westwards, 365ft (111m) above sea level, stands the **Windmill** on the highest point of the Island. The date inscribed over the door is 1571.

Island Hall

The **Island Hall**, was built by Dame Sybil to provide Islanders with recreational facilities and a meeting place. Like the church it has no particular appeal but it is at the hub of island life and there is usually something going on here to which visitors are always made welcome.

It was built by Helier de Carteret and itremained in use, grinding the corn of the Seigneur and histenants until 1919. Today, having been used as a watch tower by the Germans, the mill lacks sails. It has however, a rather ornate weather vane which the Germans did not destroy.

La Coupée

Past the mill the road runs to **La Vaurocque** crossroads and from here a straight road south will take you to La Coupée, one of the most dramatic locations in the Island. This narrow strip of land joins the larger mass of Sark with Little Sark. The strip is only as wide as a footpath and it stands 260ft (79m) above the sea. On the eastern edge of the path, there is a sheer drop to the sea and although the western edge is not sheer, it is certainly a very steep descent to the sandy beach of **Grande Grève** far below. There is a narrow footpath to take you to the beach here and a surprising number of people use it. Until 1900 there were no railings to help you across La Coupée and so at times, it was difficult to cross over the crumbling path to Little Sark. The present fencing was erected by the troops of the British liberation forces in 1945.

Little Sark

There may be a number of reasons why many visitors fail to make the crossing to Little Sark, but of those who do, many report that it is even better than its larger cousin. Reasons given include its magnificent coastline and its lack of people. Following the road from La Coupée across **Little Sark**, there is a path opposite a house called **Clos de la Pointe** which runs eastwards and drops down to **Le Pot,** a wild and beautiful part of the shore where one of Le Pelley's failed copper mines was located.

Further south along the road you'll reach **La Sablionnerie Hotel**, a delightful place in an equally delightful location. La Sablionnerie has an excellent restaurant which offers a full à la carte menu, or lighter meals and snacks in the tea gardens. There are several attractive cottages close-by known as **The Village**, and just a little way further on, **Port Gorey** lies below the site of the silver mines whose ruins can still be seen in the valley to the left. There is a good path to where the silver was loaded and shipped and it is still possible to see the chimney and the ruins of the old engine house, but the mine workings and shafts are overgrown.

By passing the mines, and following a steep path down to the water you'll arrive at the **Venus Pool**, a huge rock pool of crystal-clear water. This is an ideal location for swimming or more serious diving. The Venus Pool was the subject of a painting by William Toplis. Above the Venus Pool stands the **Point à Clouet**, an excellent place for watching the puffins nesting on the offshore rock known as **L'Etac de Serk.**

A smaller yet equally beautiful pool known as the **Pool of Adonis**, can be reached after a long climb from the cliffs beyond the village cottages. The views from this southern tip of Sark are outstanding.

The South Coast

The only way to return from Little Sark is to retrace your steps over La Coupée. Once back on the main island however, you can vary your journey back to the Avenue by taking a rather obscure turning to the right after climbing up from La Coupée.

This little path takes you along the summit of the cliffs and on to the **Dixcart Hotel** set in truly beautiful surroundings at the approach to **Dixcart Valley**. From here the path follows a stream through the woods to **Dixcart Bay**, one of the most popular spots in the Island.

On the left is the headland of **Pointe Chateau**, where a French fort once stood. It is easily reached from **La Collinette** crossroads in the Village, by walking south past the house called **La Peigneurie** and descending towards **Petit Dixcart**. A path on the left then takes you along the **Hog's Back**, a fine ridge which separates **Derrible Bay** and Dixcart. Pointe Château is at the extreme tip where an old gun lies pointing out to sea.

La Coupée which connects Sark with Little Sark; and the beach below La Grande Grêve

Chimneys above the silver mines, Little Sark

Silver mines, Little Sark

Venus Pool, Little Sark

Derrible Bay

On your return, providing it isn't high tide when the sea covers part of the path, you can visit Derrible Bay by following a steep track down from the Hog's Back. Initially the path descends through a copse and then after a short way, it takes you right to the brink of **Le Creux du Derrible**. Be careful here, the aperture is unfenced and the drop to sea level is sheer.

Le Creux du Derrible is a remarkable natural feature standing 180ft (55m) above the beach. It comprises a shaft or chimney rising from a double-entrance cave which can be easily reached from the sandy bay. It is an awesome sight, no matter whether you view it from the top or from its base on the beach. Swimming in Derrible Bay is good, and it has a good stretch of sand and several interesting caves to explore.

Point Derrible, the bay's eastern headland is best viewed from a boat. It is a difficult and dangerous place to visit in any other way.

The East Coast

A leisurely trip from La Collinette crossroads down Rue Lucas and a right turn towards the Mermaid Tavern, is the key to exploring the northern and eastern shores and cliffs. A path from just beyond the Mermaid takes you to the **Lighthouse**, which is visible from the ferry just before it enters the harbour. Turn left and then right along the path after the Mermaid and the way will lead to **Point Robert**. From here there is a flight of steps down to the Lighthouse.

Retrace your steps back past the Mermaid to Rue Lucas and turn right along the road. This leads to **La Ville Roussel,** where you'll find a collection of houses including one or two which are clearly very old indeed. From here there is a lane running eastwards towards the cliffs. A winding path from here takes you down to **Grève de la Ville**.

Beyond La Ville Roussel, the **Rue du Fort** takes you to **La Tour,** a settlement partly enclosed by grassy walls, which were clearly part of some old defence work. There is a path from here which leads down an attractive valley to **La Banquette Landing**.

Just a little way further along Rue du Fort, there is **Le Fort Farm**, and close-by there are footpaths leading eastwards to **Creux Belet**, a huge gash in the island's coastline, and rocky **Les Fontaines Bay**.

The North

Back on Rue du Fort, the road from Le Fort Farm turns westward and, after a short distance, it joins the **Eperquerie Road.** A left turn here takes you back inland towards the Seigneurie and on towards the village. A right turn however, leads to **L'Eperquerie Common,** and as the land slopes away, there is a well made path down to the landing. Boats would be moored here in the days when fishing was a major activity for Islanders.

There is an old upturned cannon overlooking the landing and at first glance you would imagine it to be one of those which were placed on headlands as part of the Island's defences against Napoleon's France. This one is different, however. It is salvage, from

Gulls' Chapel

Nearby is La Chapelle des Mauvres, (Gulls' Chapel). It is, in fact, nothing more than an arched rock, although some people have stated that its shape has a 'chapel-like' appearance. This bay is best visited in the morning when it gains the benefit of full sun. Occasionally, you'll see one of the ferries temporarily moored here, although often skippers prefer to make use of other moorings which have been laid in Dixcart Bay.

asailing vessel, the *Valentine*, an East Indiaman wrecked off the island of Brecqhou in 1781.

Les Boutiques and Le Nez

Climbing back along the path towards the road, there is a turning to the right (northwards), which takes you towards the **Butts** where the militia undertook target practice. Before reaching them however, climb down the sinister looking gully on your left. A short distance down on the right, you'll find the entrance to **Les Boutiques**. These caves are easy to explore without the need for a torch.

Some say that they were named from the French word for a shop or a store because they were used as warehouses by smugglers. Others doubt this, pointing out that there are far better places to store goods than in these caves but despite this, stories of pirates and smugglers remain and the reputation of Les Boutiques and has not faded.

Like all caves, they are best explored at low tide. The more northerly of Le Boutiques ends in a gully, from where it is possible to scramble up to the path leading to Sark's most northerly point, **Le Nez**.

Beyond Le Nez, there is a chain of rocks and islets which can be reached at low water. The first, **La Grune** is an enormous grass-covered rock. Beyond La Grune stands **La Corbée du Nez** and then **Le Bec du Nez**.

On the headland, above Les Boutiques by the L'Eperquerie path, there is a square fort built by the French during the sixteenth century. There is an eighteenth century gun here. Close-by there is another footpath leading roughly south eastwards towards **Les Fontaines Bay**.

Here, if you are familiar with the works of the artist, **William Toplis**, you'll find the **Fairy Grotto** which appears in his painting. Find the right position, when looking through two natural arches, and with luck and a good deal of imagination, you'll see the shape of a woman formed in the rock – presumably she is the fairy.

La Seigneurie

This is the central attraction on the Island. It stands on the site of St Magloire's Monastery which was sacked by Norse raiders in the ninth century, leaving little but a pile of stones. Today it is the private and official residence of the Seigneur and therefore it is not open to the public, but it can be viewed at close quarters when the grounds and walled gardens are open each Monday and Wednesday.

Despite the mild, virtually frost free climate, Sark can be a hostile environ-

Vraic

The use of 'Vraic' as a fertiliser on farmland is common throughout the Channel Islands. Huge amounts of brown seaweed are deposited on the beaches in autumn, especially after periods of stormy weather. It seems to work well as a fertiliser despite the huge amounts of salt which it must contain. Collecting, carting and spreading vraic over the fields, is a traditional autumn activity among the farming communities of the Channel Islands.

Dixcart Bay

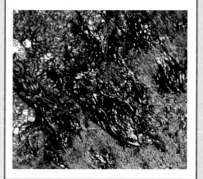

The hole in the rock and the magnificent view at the end

Sark's Unique Ambulance

As a visitor to the Island, it is sometimes easy to forget that this picture-postcard place is also a living and working community, relatively isolated from many of the utilities and services which we take for granted. In winter for example, it can be an isolated spot. The small motorboat which provides a link with Guernsey has to be cancelled occasionally as storms roll into the Western Approaches and up channel from the Atlantic, so experienced Islanders have to stockpile essential provisions and plan well ahead.

This sense of isolation has been enhanced by the Islanders' brave decisions to avoid the environmental damage which some of the so called 'benefits' of the twentieth century would have on their tiny island.

Sark has **no airport**, and considering that its residents won't even allow a motor car to be driven here, it is highly unlikely that the Island will ever build one. On Sark, the term 'horsepower' retains its original meaning. The only petrol-driven machines you are likely to find here are farmers' tractors.

So, how does the community cope with things which cannot be foreseen. What about illness, accident and health care for example?

There is a **doctor** on the Island, but the nearest hospital is at St Peter Port in Guernsey. Patients can be taken there by **water ambulance** from Sark's tiny harbour but, for an island with such strict rules about motor vehicles, it could be difficult transporting sick or injured Islanders from their isolated farmsteads to the harbour. Fortunately, Islanders have solved the problem of how to provide an ambulance without breaking the law. They purchased the rear end of a conventional ambulance and fitted a tow hitch at the front. These days the doctor visits his patients by tractor and, if required, he can hitch the ambulance onto the tow-bar behind!

ment for many types of vegetation which suffer the damage that strong winds and a salt laden atmosphere can inflict. So the high walls of the **Seigneurie Gardens** are the key to preserving the lush vegetation to be found inside. Many half hardy plants, usually seen only in greenhouses, flourish here within the protection the walls offer. The gardens really must be seen.

The Seigneurie is one of the most beautiful manor houses in the Channel Islands. It dates back to 1675 when it was originally known as **La Perronerie**. It has been the residence of the Seigneur since 1730 when Susanne, on becoming the Dame of Sark, decided to continue living here rather than move to the Manoir which was the original manor house. Having made her decision, she gave Le Manoir to the church minister.

Some argue that the architecture of the Seigneurie was spoiled in 1854 by the Collings family; they succeeded the Le Pelley's as Seigneurs and built a **signal tower** so that they could send and receive visual messages from members of the family in Guernsey. Dame Sybill Hathaway wanted to demolish it when she became the Dame, but discovered that it would be a prohibitively expensive undertaking.

Standing by the house there is an ornate **dovecote tower**, built in 1733 to house Dame Susanne Le Pelley's pigeons. It now provides a home to the present Seigneur's flock of white fan-tailed doves. Also beside the residence, there are two former chapels. One is believed to be medieval.

Close by is a path which leads to the battery where, among more modern ordnance, there is a bronze 'saker' which Queen Elizabeth I presented to Helier de Carteret. The original carriage rotted away a long time ago, and the carriage you see today is made of timber taken from *HMS Victory*.

Other items of interest within the grounds are some relics of the German occupation and a granite cider crusher. Also there are usually some farm animals to be seen, including cattle tethered in the traditional way.

Port du Moulin

Leaving the grounds by the old archway, you can gain access to the west of the Island by walking a few yards to the north and then turning left by the house called **L'Ecluse**. This road takes you down to Port du Moulin but before you reach the beach, look out for the **Window in the Rock**, a massive opening in the cliff face which was made in the nineteenth century to enable vraic (seaweed) to be collected from the beach for use as fertiliser.

By standing at the right spot, the window can provide a wonderful 'framed' view of north-western Sark, but take care at the seaward end, it is a long and dangerous drop to sea level. The flat space close to the window is thought to have been the site of the monastery watermill (moulin in French) which gave this bay its name.

Access to the beach is through a natural arch. When the tide is right, you can reach **Les Autelets,** huge rocks which provide homes for scores of kittiwakes. Locally these stacks are known as **the little altars**, probably because of their flat tops. This is a fascinating beach, but take care, keep aclose eye on the state of the tide: the cliffs are sheer and the only way back is through the arch.

On your return to L'Ecluse from the beach, it is possible to follow the cliff path northwards for a little way to a magnificent viewpoint above the Autelet Stacks. It's a pleasant path, and from here you can make yourway back La Seigneurie.

The West Coast

Longue Pointe above Havre Gosselin is one of the real gems of the Island. It is easy to get to from La Collinette: simply walk or ride to La Vaurocque crossroads and carry on westwards. The lane leads to a fork in the road and a collection of buildings, and a duck-pond, known as **Beauregard**. The Hotel Beauregard is a pleasant place to stop for refreshments.

To the west you'll find a stone obelisk, the **Pilcher Monument,** towering over the cliffs, in memory of Jeremiah Pilcher, one of a group of people who drowned when their boat was overtaken by foul weather while attempting to sail to Guernsey from here in 1868.

Far below the obelisk, there is **Havre Gosselin,** a beautiful tiny natural harbour which is rarely used today. The pathway down is steep, but safe and easy to use. Unfortunately, because it zig zags, the view deteriorates as you descend. Surprisingly therefore, the best view of Havre Gosselin is your initial view − from the top.

Fishing is not so important these days and anyway, skippers are much more likely to use Maseline or Creux. Sometimes however, you'll find an occasional pleasure boat in there, with the crew swimming in the clear water or barbecuing on the shore.

In the harbour you'll find an iron ladder rising to the cliff path from the depths of the water. Until 1912, when the quay and steps were built, this ladder was the only landing-place. You'll notice it slopes outwards slightly, making boarding and disembarking difficult in any kind of swell. Across the inlet you'll see **Telegraph Bay** on Guernsey, where the cable used to run from.

A short walk beyond the obelisk takes you to **Longue Pointe.** From here you have a view of Brecqhou in the foreground, the other islands in the distance, Havre Gosselin and the Gouliot Caves close by, Le Nez to the north and the beautiful cliffs of western Sark to the south.

Caves

The **Victor Hugo Caves** are beneath Longue Pointe. They were named by him when he visited the Island. They're best viewed from the sea, but they are not the most spectacular caves on the Island.

For the everyday visitor, these are to be found at **Les Gouliots**, not far from here. To see them, retrace your steps to **Beauregard** and follow the path westwards from **Petit Beauregard**, a house well known for the beauty of its garden. The path leads to a rocky headland overlooking the **Gouloit Passage**, a narrow stretch of water which separates Sark from Brecqhou.

Once you've taken in the view, continue on down the path to the first cave known as **The Chimney.** This

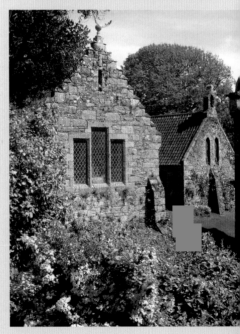

La Seigneurie, Sark

Brecqhou

As you approach Sark, the tiny privately-owned island of **Brecqhou** stands in front of the main mass of the island. Brecqhou is noticeable for the conspicuous yet mysterious fairy-tale castle which the Barclay brothers have recently built there. They shy away from intrusion and publicity, so what the castle contains or why they chose to build it there remains a mystery. Enquiries by the press have met a wall of silence and, at times, speculation has driven the brothers to preserve their privacy by taking legal actions against the media.

The Barclays

Brecqhou is now privately owned, so it cannot be visited – only viewed from Sark or the sea. The island was sold for £3,000 by Dame Sibyl Hathaway in 1929, and the new owner was given a seat on the Chief Pleas.

Brecqhou came up for sale again in 1993 and was bought by the Barclay brothers, David and Frederick, for £2.3 million.

These identical twins started their working lives as housepainters in England and amassed a fortune in real estate. Now, among other things, they own the Barclay Hotel Group and several newspapers, including *The Scotsman*. Together, they are reputed to be worth more than a billion dollars.

The Barclays avoid publicity however, so speculation about them tends to fill the gap in local knowledge. It is known however, that they both have wives and four grown children between them. According to their official photograph, they part their hair on opposite sides. Otherwise they are indistinguishable.

The brothers' private helicopter is frequently used to assist in local search and rescue operations.

Cruise around Sark

Given several days of settled weather, there are few trips in the Channel Islands which can be as exciting and interesting as a small boat trip around Sark. These expeditions are led by highly knowledgeable local small boat skippers, who take you right into the caves and gullies whenever the weather permits. Even on calm sunny days however, a sea swell, often caused by poor weather several hundreds of miles away, can make entering some places difficult and dangerous, so each boat trip is unique. You visit only the places which weather conditions allow.

Given ideal conditions, a typical trip will take the best part of a day, so make sure to have food and refreshments with you. Trips usually leave **Maseline** or **Creux Harbour** and sail north or south depending on the weather.

From the start, it will become clear that views of Sark from the sea are very different to those you obtain from vantage points high above. From a small boat, there are so many caves to be seen that they cannot all be listed or named. Secret beaches feature heavily too, many of which are inaccessible from above and so truly belong to the kingdom of the sea.

At times, the deep water passages take you so close inshore that you feel you could almost step off the boat without getting your feet wet. Even people with no particular interest in caves or seabirds will be impressed by the fantastic rock structures, columns, stacks and natural arches.

A Clockwise Voyage

On a south-about trip, things start to get exciting almost immediately as **Cathedral Cave** comes into view by the **Lâches** moorings, followed by **Dungeon Cave** in Petit Derrible Bay.

Beyond Derrible Bay there is the **Convanche Chasm,** between Dixcart and La Coupée. It has a blow hole and a small entrance leading to a tunnel in which there is deep, clear, still water – an eerie spot.

Past La Coupée and the isolated inaccessible beach there on its eastern shore, boatmen often pause for a while to allow passengers to take in the rugged beauty of **Le Pot** in **Little Sark**. From here, the boat heads offshore to call at **L'Etac de Serk**, a great rock to the south of the island, covered in flowers and home to huge flocks of seabirds.

Further round the Island, boats usually pass the great rock **La Moie de Gorey**, and then sail into **Port Gorey** where the silver mining used to take place. There are spectacular rocks all around at this point in the voyage, especially off **Les Fontaines Bay.** Just beyond, you arrive at the western side of La Coupée. Usually there are people on the beach here at **Grande Grève,** and high above you may see people leaning on the fence, peering down at you from the causeway which connects Sark with Little Sark. Next comes **Port es Saies**, one of those beaches which can only be reached by sea, followed by the massive cavern-pierced headland, **La Moie des Orgeries.**

Victor Hugo Cave follows. Given the right weather conditions and state of tide, the chances are that your skipper will take you in here.

Next comes **Havre Gosselin**, a natural harbour with caves all around and the **Pilcher Monument** towering high overhead, a reminder that these waters are not always so benign and picture-postcard perfect. Sailing on from here, the mystery of Brecqhou, the island which no-one may visit, draws everyone's attention, and the spectacular cliffs and caves are of major interest.

The most spectacular part of the trip however, is here in **Le Gouliot Passage** where the boat sails through the great square-mouthed cave entrance to enter **Port a la Jument.** Then comes the crag of **Tintageu**, close to the **Port du Moulin**, with its natural arch and sheer cliffs, above which are the woods of the Seigneurie grounds.

Following Port du Moulin, the boat takes you past **Les Autelets** and into **Suignie Bay** where there is yet another large cave with a blow-hole. Whether it is working will depend upon the state of the tide. Next comes a chain of rocks known as **Les Sept Moies** before the mouths of the **Boutiques** caves come into view.

Once round **La Pointe du Nez** comes **L'Eperquerie,** the original landing place of the 1563 settlers and then the boat arrives at the yawning entrance to **Creux Belet** on Sark's eastern coast. Close by there is the **Red Cave**, famed for its small entrance and vast interior. After **Point Banquette, Point Robert Lighthouse** situated half-way up the cliff comes into view and the end of the voyage is in sight. There is still one more surprise however: The **Dog Cave**, famed for its double aperture and named after the barking noise which the sea makes as it enters its resonant chambers.

cave leads on into the vast main cavern from which you can gain a view of the sea through apertures in the rock. For serious explorers, prepared for scrambling and wading, there are various other caverns leading off from this main one which can be visited. The best is the **Anemone Cave** entered through a split arch. Its walls are completely covered by variously coloured anemones and 'dead mens fingers'. Given the right state of tide, somepeople enjoy swimming in the subterranean pools.

This whole complex of caves is both spectacular and eerie. It is perfectly safe to visit them providing you are dressed appropriately, take a torch, and are sure of the state of tide. Obviously low water springs is the best time, when the greatest part of the complex is exposed.

Brecqhou

With an area of only 165 acres, Brecqhou lies across the **Gouliot Passage** beyond **Le Moie de Gouliot,** a rock stack towering out of the water. The name implies a 'break' or a 'severance', probably a reference to the fact that Brecqhou is isolated from Sark by these fierce waters.

In many respects, the Island is a miniature model of Sark. It has the same tableland plateau and similar cliffs and caves. **Le Port**, Brecqhou's tiny harbour with its equally tiny pier, is at the opposite side of the Island facing Guernsey in the west. There is another landing place, **Galet de Jacob**, on the northern coast.

The Island seems to have been almost constantly occupied, although the number of inhabitants at any one time was probably small. Copper mining

---

Visiting Caves

If you are unsure about visiting caves alone, or if you wish to do some more serious caving around the Island's coast, it is advisable to employ a local guide. Terrance Kiernan, author of the book *Caves and Scrambles of Sark* is such a person. Proceeds from his activities on the Island are used to fund a number of projects in India. Terrance makes the point that some of Sark's caves are difficult to access, there are no paths and no electric lights within them. Many of them fill up with sea water at every high tide so it makes sense to use a local expert. Terrance supplies all the necessary equipment except mountain boots or shoes.

---

was tried here during the nineteenth century, but the workings were abandoned due to constant flooding.

Since purchasing the Island, the Barclays have spent upward of £25 million in constructing the largest castle built in the twentieth century, a controversial turreted Gothic structure with 100 foot high granite walls.

In the absence of hard facts, the locals can only speculate about what was installed there, or indeed what goes on behind those massive granite walls. The best and most reasonable guess however, seems to be that the castle comprises self-contained homes for individual family members within the four towers:– a library, a games room, two indoor swimming pools, a chapel and a weatherproof atrium. There is also a helipad.

It has been reported that the brothers are mounting a legal challenge to Sark's jurisdiction over Brecqhou, in particular, they object to Sark's feudal inheritance laws.

This has led to a complex and long running legal battle in which the Crown and UK government have been placed in a situation where they are defending Sark's right to maintain it's feudal laws, despite the fact that these laws fly in the face of all UK equal opportunity policy and legislation. The outcome may be far-reaching for Europe's last feudal stronghold, but judgement is not expected for a few years yet!

Leaving Sark

There is only one way to leave the Island, and this entails a return trip down the hill to Maseline Harbour. The toast rack public transport usually operates from the **Bel Air** tavern to carry passengers back in time for sailings but the footpath down the valley side to the harbour offers the opportunity for a pleasant stroll at the end of a perfect day.

The chances are that you'll want to give yourself plenty of time in order not to miss your boat, but you can turn this to advantage by using the waiting time to visit **Creux Harbour** which you may not have seen yet, especially if you jumped aboard the first toast-rack up the hill after disembarking at Maseline.

Creux is at the bottom of the hill by the cafe. Rather than walking through the tunnel back to Maseline, walk through the tunnel opposite and you'll arrive at Creux, a much smaller harbour and quay constructed of red stone, a slipway and a small pebble beach. Creux was used extensively before Maseline was built, but like many Channel Island harbours it dries out at low water. These days, it is too small for the passenger ferries which ply between here and the other islands. It is still used though by visiting yachts and local boatmen.

At the top of the pebble beach, there is a third tunnel, much older than the others. It was built by Helier de Carteret. The date 1588 is carved in the granite archway at the entrance. The exit is by the cafe at the bottom of the hill, a few yards from Maseline Harbour and your ferry.

HERM AND JETHOU

Herm Seaway Express operates a fast 100-seater ferry service between Guernsey and the Island of Herm which lies about three miles to the east of Guernsey. During the summer the blue ferries leave St Peter Port every half hour from 10.00 am onwards, but there is an earlier ferry which goes to Herm to bring back the milk. Take this 'milk run' and it is possible to spend about eleven hours on the Island without resorting to an overnight stay. It is a short trip, only about twenty minutes, but to add interest to the voyage, the company takes a roundabout outward course on most of their trips, in order to bring you close to the tiny yet fascinating island of Jethou.

Outward bound, you'll thread your way through the hussle and bustle of St Peter Port Harbour passing quite close to a number of ships and fishing vessels and once outside, there are usually several other craft to be seen anchored in the roads. The water between Guernsey and Herm is known as the **Little Russel**. It is a place of strong tides and there are outcrops of rock everywhere. On the journey, you'll notice that the ferry makes several turns and twists in order to stay in the deep water channels.

Usually, ferries pass close to **Bréhon Tower**, a huge nineteenth century fortification which looks much older. Bréhon has seen little military use, although the Germans placed an anti-aircraft battery there. Today it is owned by the States and its chief purpose is as a navigational mark and a platform for a flashing light during the hours of darkness.

Herm

Just after the Second World War, the Lieutenant Governor of Guernsey, Sir Philip Neame VC, spent a couple of days on Herm and enjoyed it so much that he declared it to be 'the nearest approach to Fairyland I have ever seen'. It has also been described as 'a naturalist's dream and a family adventure playground all wrapped into one'.

On Herm there are no cars, no tarmac roads, and no traffic except a tractor or two. It is only one and a half miles long and about three quarters of a mile wide but, despite its diminutive size, Herm is an island where you can always find a quiet spot and see very few people all day. Its shape has been likened to a wedge of cheese on its side.

Geographically speaking, the overall structure is similar to that of Guernsey. Both islands have high land in the south and flatter low-lying ground to the north. It is an ideal location for sunbathing, birdwatching, walking, shell hunting, or just somewhere to sit and enjoy the peace and quiet of an unpolluted, unhurried and unspoiled natural paradise.

There is plenty of evidence to support the theory that Herm was well known to **prehistoric man**. In fact, it has been suggested that the volume of remains and the size of the prehistoric works on the Island are too large for the size of community which Herm could have supported. Could it be therefore, that Herm had a special significance at these times? Was it a **burial ground** for the illustrious dead of further afield, nearby France for example? If so, why would they go to such trouble to carry their dead here? We'll probably never know.

Religious sites

Herm has other mysteries too, and **St Tugual's Chapel** is one of them, standing on the summit of a hill overlooking the harbour. It is certainly old, mentioned in a Papal Bull of Pope Urban III in 1186, but the date when it was built is uncertain. Some suggest that it was built by **St Magloire** when he founded his religious house in Sark, and perhaps his chapel in Guernsey, during the sixth century. The real mystery however surrounds the identity of St Tugual. Who was he (or she)? Where did St Tugual come from, and what happened to him or her?

Monks inhabited Herm from time to time through its history. In fact the Island suppported a small colony of them briefly as late as the early 1880s, so it is reasonable to assume that the chapel was used, periodically at least, as a place of worship. It was restored and converted to a private chapel when Prince Blucher was the tenant of the Island, before his internment at the start of the First World War.

Today, the chapel is in excellent condition and is still used as a place of worship. The present tennant of the Island, Major Peter Woods, holds regular Sunday services there, often assisted by volunteer organists recruited from among the guests at the Island's hotel.

Industrial activities

The name 'Herm', is said to mean 'deserted' or 'uncultivated' land, a strange title for an island which, by the seventeenth century, had become the **hunting ground** of the Governors of Guernsey. Deer and rabbit were the main targets. In 1656, the historian Peter Heylin reported that Herm's main inhabitants were 'pheasants and goode plenty conies' (rabbits).

During the nineteenth century, hunting on the Island gave way to **quarrying**. For a while this was a large-scale operation. There were excavations at **La Rosière** near the present landing steps, at **Le Monceau** north of the harbour, and on the common. The work also extended to the islet of **Crevichon** just to the north of Jethou. For a while, this activity employed a considerable number of men.

By the 1830s, Herm's population was about 400, and among the buildings erected at the time, there was a small lock-up which still stands in the grounds of the **White House Hotel**, a building which also owes its existence to this period. It was the quarrying ac-tivity and the need to load and unload barges which also led to the building of Herm Harbour.

As well as quarrying, there was also an attempt made to mine **copper** on the cliffs above Le Rosière. A large investment was made but little was acheived. The industrial phase of Herm's history gradually declined as exports of granite from Guernsey and Alderney increased. The Island's remoteness from the granite's eventual destination and the opening of the new harbour in St Peter Port, finally ended the quarrying activity and led Herm into a new period when, during the latter half of the nineteenth century, it was tenanted by a series of wealthy families who did a great deal to erase the industrial scars from the landscape.

As a result of their activities the manor, once described as a 'ponderous pile', became used as a farm, and the quarrymen's simple dwellings were improved. The most opulent and famous tenant during that period was Prince Blucher.

War years

There was a small military garrison stationed on Herm during the First World War and then, in 1920, **Compton Mackenzie** rented both Herm and Jethou from the Crown. He stayed on Herm for three years before moving his residence to Jethou. While living on Herm, he allowed public access to Shell Beach. He didn't particularly welcome visitors, but he needed the money which their landing fees earned for him. A few years later he sold his lease to Sir Percival Perry who lived there until the outbreak of war in 1939.

Above: Looking at Sark from Herm

Above right, right, below: The tiny harbour and beach on Herm

Opposite: Mouisonnére Beach, Herm

Pirates and Privateers

Throughout the history of the Islands, the sea had provided income in one way or another, through fishing in peacetime and at other times through smuggling, privateering, and piracy.

Smuggling is a well-understood term, but what of 'Piracy' and 'Privateering', and what is the difference?

Piracy is the act of taking a ship on the high seas from the possession or control of those lawfully entitled to it. The key word here is 'lawfully'. Piracy is an illegal act and piracy thrives in places where international law does not prevail.

Sark, for example, was frequently used as a haven for pirates at a time when the hostilities between France and England meant that the Island was beyond the control of either power. Pirates are indiscriminate, they have no particular allegiances and are usually prepared to attack any ship which appears vulnerable.

Privateers however, were privately owned vessels armed with guns which operated at times of war against the enemy's merchant ships. The men who owned and sailed such vessels were also known as Privateers. Unlike pirates, these seamen were operating within the law, commissioned by their governments to take and destroy enemy vessels as part of the war effort.

Ships and goods known as **prizes**, taken by a privateer, were handed over to the Admiralty to be sold. The profits from such sales were then shared between the crown and the privateers.

An investment in privateering was a costly high-risk business, but profits could be astronomical, especially after 1708 when the Crown waived its right to a share. Generally speaking, the value of the prize was divided into eighths, of which three eighths went to the captain, one eighth went to the commander-in-chief, one to the officers, one to the warrant officers, and two to the crew.

Perhaps the most famous example of prize money distribution was that which went to the officers and crews of the frigates *Active* and *Favourite* following the capture of the Spanish treasure ship *Hermione* in 1762. The two captains each received £65,000 and every Lieutenant earned £13,000. Each seaman in the two ships gained £485.

The end of privateering came towards the end of the nineteenth century. Later in 1907, the **Hague Convention** stipulated that although merchant ships could be armed for self-defence, privateers should be listed as warships. The distribution of prize money to captains and crews was abolished in Britain after the Second World War.

Sir Percival established a Post Office on Herm in 1925.

During the Second World War, the Germans didn't bother to fortify the Island but they did use it as an excercise area and a place of recreation. The Island was occupied from time to time however, because the Guernsey States cultivated some of the land and grazed cattle there. In 1943 a British commando force was landed, but found the Island to be deserted.

Today Herm is owned by the States of Guernsey. It was purchased from the Crown in 1946 for £15,000 and Mr A G Jefferies became the States' first tenant on the Island, but the task of repairing five years of neglect proved to be too much for him. The present tenants are Adrian and Pennie Wood Heyworth.

Getting there

How you arrive and land on Herm depends upon the state of tide. At low water the launch stops at **Le Rosière** steps but, given sufficient rise of tide, the boat will take you into the tiny harbour with its old crane, a reminder of the days when granite was loaded onto barges here. Usually on a day trip, you'll experience both the steps and the harbour, disembarking at one location and embarking at another. The distance between them is negligible.

On arrival, the **White House Hotel** and the **Mermaid Tavern** are close-by and most visitors make a bee-line for them. As a hotel, the White House is one of the best in the Channel Islands, well known for both its comfort and quality of cuisine. **The Ship Restaurant** attached, is open to non-residents and provides excellent food at reasonable prices.

Nearby, the Mermaid Tavern stands in an attractive courtyard where you can eat, drink, and relax. As you would expect, there is good home-made pub grub here, served in quantities you'll appreciate if you've just completed a tour of the Island on foot. Close-by too, there is an excellent campsite and a row of self-catering cottages.

From here you have several options. Much of course will depend on the weather, the amount of time you have to spend on the Island and your level of energy and curiosity.

Many people head straight up the hill towards the **Manor**, the **Chapel** and **Belvoir Bay.** Others head north, taking the direct path to **Shell Beach**, Herm's most famous attraction.

A round tour of the Island

To avoid the other visitors, why not make a round tour of the Island starting northwards from the harbour? For a while you'll be walking alongside people heading directly for Shell Beach, but in a little while you'll find that you have the path pretty much to yourself. So long as you've got the sea on your left hand side, you cannot go far wrong.

Before too long you'll arrive at a very attractive fisherman's cottage, and opposite, out to sea, you'll spot the tiny islet of **Hermetier.** You can stroll out to it at low water. From here, you can continue your walk along the beach if you like, although the sand, composed largely of shell fragments, can be hard on the feet.

Inland, the ground gently rises and you'll probably see plenty of Guernsey

Le Rosière Steps

cattle grazing. Above the fisherman's cottage stands **Le Monceau**, a wooded hill which used to be the site of one of Herm's granite quarries. The steps of **St Paul's Cathedral** in London are paved with Herm granite, perhaps from Le Monceau.

A short way on, you'll discover the little **cemetery** with a cross standing over it bearing the inscription, '*In memory of K W Conden aged 2 years. R Mansfield aged 23 years. Died April 18..........*', the rest is indecipherable. No-one knows how, why or when these people died. Tradition has it that they were victims of cholera. Maybe they were Island residents.

Ahead lies the Common and the northern part of the Island. This is a real treasure trove for anyone with a liking for prehistory. The first **neolithic graves** can be seen on the slopes of a hillock known as **Le Petit Monceau** and at this stage of the journey, you'll find that the flat stones make ideal resting places.

The north

Staying by the sea however, and avoiding any right turns across the Island towards Shell Beach, you'll arrive at the north-west tip of Herm. Just offshore from here, there is a low flat islet called **Plat Houmet**, a popular spot for wildfowl and a wide variety of other birdlife.

Further away and depending on the state of the tide, you may see lots of other rocks and tiny islets. At low water, a vast expanse of sand is exposed and it is possible to walk out a long way. At low spring tides, it is even possible to walk out to the **Vermerette Beacon** which faces the harbour. Some say that there are traces of neolithic structures even here.

The northern shore of Herm is very low lying and constantly in danger of erosion. Walk along the sand of **Mouisonniere Beach** or along the footpath, but try to avoid walking along the seaward edge of the Common. The vegetation there is the major weapon in arresting erosion, but the grasses and other plants are delicate and shouldn't be stepped on. Be careful also not to stray off the path onto the Common in bare feet. The **Burnett Rose** is a common plant here and its thorns are particuarly sharp and painful.

To seaward there are lots of tiny islets known as **Les Amfrocques**. Locally they are known as **The Humps**, and at high tide they aren't much to look at, but at other states of the tide they can appear much more intersting. At one time, the Island extended beyond its present boundaries and encompassed them.

Midway along the northern shore

Left: The Ship Inn

Left middle: The gentle low lying landscape of Herm

Below: The cosy Belvoir Bay

stands **Le Pierre aux Rats**. Originally on this site stood an **ancient monolith** which had served as a seamark for centuries. Unfortunately it was destroyed by quarry-men, but their actions caused such an outcry that the quarrying company was obliged to build the present pillar as a replacement.

From **Shell Beach** you have the option of returning directly to the harbour area, or continuing on southwards along the path which runs along the base of the gentle cliffs to Belvoir Bay, described by some as the most attractive inlet in the Island. Belvoir is the ideal spot for a lazy afternoon. The sand is clean and the water here is remarkably clear.

East coast

Southwards from here, the coastal path transforms into a cliff path as you leave the flat northern area and enter the higher southern portion of this 'wedge of cheese'. Obviously, walking here is more strenuous – you pass through undergrowth, the ocassional boggy area, and patches of light woodland – but the distances are small, the path is good, and there are plenty of resting places.

The cliffs here are spectacular, especially in spring when they become the temporary home of large numbers of migrating birds. Walking southwards you have views of the sea and probably the island of Sark on your left. Below, there is an ever-changing scene of steep green slopes and tiny bays, many of which are inaccessible to anyone without a small boat. Above are the meadows which sustain Herm's herd of Guernsey cattle.

At **Le Creux Pignon,** Herm's cliffs reach their maximum height of 190ft and become sheer. Le Creux was originally a cave with an aperture in its roof. In 1964 however, the entire structure collapsed and the process of erosion hasn't finished yet. Today you'll find a strong barricade between the path and the cliff edge, to discourage anyone from exploring the area further.

The path takes you down a flight of steps to the southern tip of the Island, **Point Sauzebourge**, which looks out onto **La Percée Passage** and Jethou just across the water. North from here, following a vague path along a barbed wire fence, takes you to the entrance to the disused and dangerous unsuccessful copper mine. Visit by all means, but don't go inside. It is far better to continue on to **Rosière Cottage** and the landing steps.

Departure

Looking to seaward from the landing, you'll see two big reefs. The southern extremity of the farthest one is known as **Gate Rock.** Watch carefully as a ferry passes it and you may notice that the rock has a small hole in it. Some say that this rock was a gatepost in the days when the Island was considerably bigger than it is today. A more likely explanation however, is that it was used as a boat mooring in the days when granite barges were regular visitors to the Island.

It's pleasant to sit on the old stone quay and wait for the ferry to take you back to Guernsey. Alternatively, with time on your hands, you could do what a large number of other visitors do and head for the **Mermaid Tavern** to enjoy a cool drink.

JETHOU

From here, the ferry turns for Jethou. Having an area of only 100 acres, this island is much smaller than Herm but it is higher, with cliffs rising to 100m (268ft) in places. The ferry passes to the south of the Island and then runs close in along Jethou's eastern shore and then northwards through the **La Percée Passage** between Jethou and Herm before arriving at Herm's tiny harbour.

It is a fascinating trip, especially as you pass close by the **Creux du Diable** (Devil's Hole). This used to be a fine blow-hole, but seepage from the land and the force of the sea in the cave over the years has changed its shape. It was also once known as 'the place of roaring' – somewhere to be avoided by ordinary folk or anyone with a sense of imagination.

In the eighteenth century however, smugglers found that it offered an ideal 'cover' for their business. They could store contraband there before taking it on to Guernsey or England. It was perfectly safe because the Creux du Diable's reputation was such that no-one was going to visit.

Nearby there is a raised beach, revealing a shoreline high above the present level. The terraced hillsides you'll see from the ferry suggest that at some time long forgotten, these slopes were cultivated. A standing stone in the **Fairy Wood** on the north face of the island, also adds weight to the argument that Jethou was populated during prehistoric times.

For such a tiny place, its history seems to be particularly macabre.

Early references record that Robert, Duke of Normandy, gave the Island to Restald, his master of shipping in 1032. Restald was a man of religious inclination who became a monk and bequeathed the Island to the Abbey of Mont St Michel. Ownership transferred to the Crown in 1416 however, when all alien religious houses were suppressed.

For many years, Jethou was associated with **smuggling**, and for a while the authorities hanged felons, freebooters, murderers and sheepstealers on gibbets on the summit of Jethou to rot away in the wind as a warning to evildoers. It is said that the corpses could be seen from the decks of sailing vessels passing between Jersey and Guernsey.

It was all to no avail however, as even as late as 1867, the then tennant of the Island, a certain Colonel Fielding, had his lease terminated after being caught red-handed using Jethou to store brandy en-route from France to England.

Islets

There are two small rocky islets close to Jethou. **Le Grande Fauconniere** is a rugged stack just off the south east coast. It is an important navigational mark, and as such, its top has been white-washed.

To the north of Jethou the cone-shaped islet of **Crevichon** cannot be mistaken. Stone was taken from here to build St Peter Port Harbour during the nineteenth century. Both islets are teaming with wildfowl and they are accessible at low water but, like Jethou, they are not open to visitors and this is as close as you get. As you circumnavigate the Island, keep a close eye on the

Shell Beach

The north eastern corner of the Island is reached at **La Point du Gentil-homme** and from here the path turns south along the edge of Shell Beach, a flat and, at first glance, rather uninteresting shoreline, which disguises one the the Channel Islands' most interesting locations.

The fascination begins the minute you sit on the beach and gather a portion of it in your hands. Look closely – this isn't sand. It is, in fact, an assortment of shell fragments which you are holding and probably a few whole ones too. This entire beach is composed of shells or bits of them, carried here from far and wide by the strong Channel Island currents and deposited uniquely on this beach.

Some are fairly common: cockels, whelks and clams etc, but others are quite rare. Armed with a good reference book, you can spend a good deal of time here. Swimming from the beach is excellent, and in summer there is a refreshment kiosk too.

Just inland, **Le Grand Monceau** stands high above Shell Beach. On its summit there is yet further evidence of neolithic activity on the Island. There were even more neolithic remains here before the quarrymen arrived and destroyed them. What remains of the site has been studied and the arte-facts are now on display in the **Guernsey Museum** in St Peter Port.

The House on Jethou

The House on Jethou dates back to the eighteenth century. It was built by John Allaire, a successful privateer who probably built on the same site as that chosen by Restauld.

In the 1890s, evidence of strange goings-on in Jethou emerged during renovations to the house. One internal wall was found to have a layer of banknotes papered beneath the outer wallpaper – almost certainly hidden profits from smuggling.

For seven years, it was the home of Compton Mackenzie who moved there in 1923 and stayed for seven years. He is best remembered as the author of *Whiskey Galore,* the tale of a small Scottish island community who 'salvaged' a cargo of whiskey from a ship stranded and wrecked just offshore. *Fairy Gold*, another Compton Mackenzie book, is charmingly set in Herm and Jethou, but both islands are given ficticious names.

The last tenant was Sir Charles Hayward who died in 1983.

shore. With luck, and in the right season, you'll see cormorants, oystercatchers and guillemots, as well as colonies of the increasingly rare **puffin**, the clown of the seas, which in recent years has almost been adopted as the 'Channel Island bird'. Herm Seaways has the Puffin as its mascot, and Channel TV also has 'Oscar Puffin' as a popular children's character.

Right: Jethou seen from above Rosiére Steps

Jethou can be seen in the centre and Herm behind

If making a call from outside Guernsey please pre-fix all listed telephone numbers with the area code 01481

Currency

Throughout the Channel Islands you will experience no problem in purchasing goods and services with UK money. The chances are, though, you'll receive Channel Island notes and coins in your change. Both Jersey and Guernsey mint their own.

With the introduction of decimalisation, coins were minted in cupro-nickel. The £1.00 coin is unpopular and as a result it is rarely seen. Instead, the green one pound note is still very much in circulation within the Islands. On occasion, special crown pieces are issued to commemorate auspicious events.

Guernsey and Jersey notes and coins have the same value as UK currency, and both currencies are acceptable through the Islands. In Guernsey, you may frequently obtain Jersey currency in your change. Don't worry, so long as you are in the Islands it will be acceptable. Island money is not acceptable in the UK however. Best advice is spend it in the islands or change it at a bank before you leave.

Finally, on the subject of money, check your notes carefully and make a point of looking at the value. Island notes are coloured differently to those of the UK, but occasionally there are similarities between the colour of notes – but not their values. In effect, the colour may seem familiar, but the value may be different – always look at the number on the note before you hand it over, or you may be giving a much larger tip than you realise.

Both Guernsey and Jersey also issue their own postage stamps.

Getting there

By air

There are frequent direct flights to Guernsey from a wide range of UK and European airports. Belfast, Birmingham, Bristol, Bournemouth, Dublin, East Midlands, Exeter, Geneva, London, Manchester, Plymouth and Southampton. Flight times from Southampton and London are under an hour, for Manchester you can expect to be in the air for about one hour and fifteen minutes.

Flights to Alderney

It is possible to fly direct from Southampton to Alderney with 'Aurigny', Alderney's own airline and Bournemouth with Blue Islands. This company also operates a number of inter-island routes and between the Islands and France.

By sea

Condor Ferries Ltd operates a regular and frequent service from Poole, Weymouth and Guernsey. The service carries both car and foot passengers aboard high speed 'Wave-piercer' catamarans which make the crossing in about two and a half hours. There is a duty free shop on board and drinks and light meals are available on each crossing.

Accommodation

There are nearly 400 establishments in Guernsey which offer accommodation. The Tourist Board grades all hotels according to a Star System:

Five Star Hotels

All bedrooms must be equipped with ensuite facilities, direct dial telephone and colour TV. There must be an extensive table d'hote and à la carte menu available. The hotel must have a full liquour licence and room service must be available at all times. Five Crown hotels also have uniformed porters on duty at all times.

Four Star Hotels

All bedrooms must be equipped with ensuite facilities, direct-dial telephone and colour TV. They must also offer half-board terms (bed, breakfast and evening meal) and a full à la carte menu. They must provide full room service from 7 am to 11 pm, together with day and night porterage.

Three Star Hotels

Ninety per cent of bedrooms must provide ensuite facilities and they must offer half-board or bed-and-breakfast. Colour TV must be provided in guest rooms and either tea / coffee-making facilities must be provided in guest rooms or, alternatively, room service must be available.

Two Star Hotels

Sixty per cent of bedrooms must provide ensuite facilities. There must be half-board or bed-and-breakfast terms offered, and facilities must be available and accessible throughout the day and evening from 8 am to 11 pm. Two Crown hotels are also required to provide service for guests arriving or departing outside of these hours.

One Star Hotels

Thirty per cent of bedrooms must provide ensuite facilities and half-board or bed-and-breakfast terms must be offered. Facilities must be available and accessible throughout the day and evening from 8am to 11pm and service must be provided for guests arriving or departing outside of these hours.

Guesthouses

Each guesthouse must usually offer at least six bedrooms and there should be a general bathroom and toilet for every six rooms which do not have their own private facilities.

The authorities also require guesthouse owners to provide the use of a telephone, ensure that the exterior of their property is well maintained, that the kitchens are clean and hygenic and that the furnishings are of good standard. Guesthouses are graded by diamonds rather than stars. Basic accommodation earns 1 diamond, 5 diamonds are the highest grade. A courteous friendly service is expected and all guesthouses should provide a full English breakfast.

Here is a sample of accommodation available. Further details and up-to-date vacancy information is available from the Tourist Board

Hotels

If making a call from outside Guernsey please pre-fix all listed telephone numbers with the area code 01481

La Barbarie Hotel (3 star)
Saints Bay, St Martin
☎ 235217
www.labarbariehotel.com

Hotel De Beauvoir (2 star)
Rue Cohu, Castel
☎ 254750

Hotel Bon Port (3 star)
Moulin Huet Bay, St Martin
☎ 239249
www.bonport.com

Le Chêne Hotel (2 star)
Forest
☎ 235566
www.lechene.co.uk

Les Cordeliers Hotel (1 star)
Les Gravees, St Peter Port
☎ 720176
www.lescordeliershotel.com

Fermain Valley Hotel (4 star)
Fermain Lane, St Peter Port
☎ 235666
www.fermainvalley.com

Fleur du Jardin (3 star)
Kings Mills Castel
☎ 257996
www.fleurdujardin.com

Old Government House Hotel (4 star)
St Peters Port
☎ 724921
www.theoghhotel.com

St Pierre Park Hotel (3 star)
Rohais, St Peters Port
☎ 728282
www.stpierrepark.com

St Martin's Country Hotel
(2 star)
Les Merriennes, St Martin
☎ 235644

Guest Houses

Anneville Guest House
(3 diamonds)
St Saviours
☎ 263814

Auberge Du Val (4 diamonds)
Sous L'Eglise, St Saviour
☎ 263862

Castaways Guest House
(2 diamonds)
Bon Port, St Martin
☎ 239010

Maison Bel Air Guest House
(4 diamonds)
Le Chene, Forest
☎ 238503
www.maisonbelair.com

St George's Hotel (3 diamonds)
St George's Esplanade, St Peter Port
☎ 721027
www.stgeorges-guernsey.com

Self Catering

A wide range of self-catering accommodation is available both as apartments, and as 'annexes' to hotels.

Beau Vallon Holiday Homes (3 star)
Les Adams, St Peters
☎ 265888

Grange Lodge Hotel Self Catering Flats
(3 star & 2 star)
The Grange, St Peter Port
☎ 725161

La Madeleine Holiday Apartments
(4 star & 3 star)
St Peters Port
☎ 726933

La Pompe Country Apartments (5 star)
Ruette de la Pompe, St Martin
☎ 239096

Camping

Caravans are not allowed into the Island but there are several campsites for tents

La Fauxquets Valley
Castel
☎ 255460

La Bailloterie
Vale
☎ 243636

Le Vaugrat
St Sampson
☎ 257468

Customs and Excise

Your duty free allowance is:

> 200 cigarettes or
> 100 cigarillos or
> 50 cigars or
> 250 grams tobacco.

Two litres of still table wine. One litre of alcoholic drink if over 22% by volume, or two litres of fortified wine, sparkling wine or liqueurs also 66cc/ml perfume or 250cc/ml toilet water.
Gifts or souvenirs up to the value of £145.00

Disabled facilities

The Island Tourist Authority is keen to ensure that all visitors enjoy their stay in the Island. A free booklet is available called 'Access in Guernsey'. It is a very comprehensive guide to special amenities in the Island. It details information on where to stay and visit and gives hints and advice on travel, toilets etc. You can obtain the booklet from: The Guernsey Tourist Board, PO Box 23, St Peter Port, Guernsey C.I. GY1 3AN. ☎ 723552. www. guernseytouristboard.com

Driving

The following information highlights the differences between driving in Guernsey and driving in the United Kingdom.

Yellow STOP lines.

A yellow line across the exit of a minor road means STOP and give way to traffic on the major road.

Yellow Arrows

A Yellow arrow painted on the road gives warning of a yellow line ahead.

The FILTER IN TURN system

Some junctions have 'FILTER IN TURN' on a sign and painted on the road. Approach them with care: the sign indicates that all directions have equal priority. You must only enter the junction in turn with other vehicles. They are also box junctions, so you must not enter the box unless your exit is clear.

Maximum speed

The maximum speed limit in the island is 35 mph (56 kph) but there are lower speed limits in some areas. In and around the town the speed limit is 25 mph (40 kph). These are maximum speeds and in many places much lower speeds are necessary for safe driving.

Accidents

Accidents involving personal injury or serious damage must be reported to the Police within 24 hours. Minor accidents not involving injury need not be reported, provided the names and addresses of those concerned are exchanged.

Yellow NO WAITING lines

A single yellow line painted along the side of the road or pavement means that you can neither park nor wait there at any time.

Parking at night

Vehicles parked at night must show lights unless they are parked in a disc zone or approved parking place. Single parking lights are not allowed.

Seat belts

Drivers and front-seat passengers must, by law, wear seat belts. Children should wear a restraint appropriate for their age.

Eating out

In Guernsey there is almost certainly a restaurant to suit your price and pallet. The enjoyment of eating out, however, is a highly personal pleasure, made even more complicated by the fact that restaurants can change their quality and style almost overnight. This list is based upon the author's experience. It is not exhaustive.

Absloute End
Longstore, St Peter Port.
Seafood specialists – waterfront dining
☎ 723822

La Barbarie Hotel
Saints Bay, St Martin.
AA Rosette Award – teas by the pool
☎ 235217

Café du Moulin
St Peter
Near restored water mill, innovative menu
using own organic produce
☎ 265944

Courts Restaurant
Le Marchant, St Peter Port
Charcoal grill, lively yet intimate.
☎ 721782

Christie's Brasserie and Bar
Le Pollet, St Peter Port
Late breakfasts, evening dinners, live jazz in
the evenings.
☎ 726624

Crabby Jack's Bistro
Vazon Bay – across the road from the beach.
Snacks or full meals, dancing at weekends.
☎ 257489

Côbo Bay Hotel, Côbo
French cuisine at its best. Eat and watch the
sun go down over the sea. Spectacular food,
spectacular sunsets!
☎ 257102

Le Nautique
Quay Steps, St Peter Port
Old seafront warehouse, popular with locals.
☎ 712714

La Grande Mare
Vazon Bay
Top Egon Ronay-rated hotel in Guernsey.
Four star luxury.
☎ 256576

Longfrie Inn
Route du Longfrie, St Peter Port
Excellent value bar lunches
and evening meals, children welcome and
catered for.
Popular family destination.
☎ 263107

Moore's Hotel
High St, St Peter Port
Excellent carvery in the library bar.
☎ 724452

Cafe Renoir
St Pierre Park Hotel
St Peter Port
☎ 728282

The Taste of India
Mill St, St Peter Port
Egon Ronay recommended
☎ 723730

The Waterfront,
North Esplanade, St Peter Port
Steaks, ribs, seafood and salads
☎ 721503

Sawatdi Thai Restaurant
North Plantation, St Peter Port
☎ 725805

Emergency services

Dial 999 as UK

Hospital

Princess Elizabeth La Vauquiedor, St Peter Port.
☎ 725241

Medical care

The Reciprocal Health Agreement between the UK and the Channel Islands ended on 31st March 2009. All visitors to the Bailiwick of Guernsey, which includes Alderney, are advised to take out full travel insurance to cover the cost of any medical treatment that they may require and repatriation costs. For summertime visitors the Healthcare Group operates a morning surgery at the Pier Steps (below Boots), St Peter Port. ☎ 711237.

Entertainment

Theatrical

A variety of theatrical performances are staged at Beau Sejour throughout the year.
☎ 747200

Cinema

The Mallard Cinema
☎ 266366
www.mallardcinema.co.uk

Nightclubs

There are a number of nightclubs in Guernsey.

Follies
The North Plantation
St Peter Port
☎ 722544

Club 54
Above the Golden Monkey
Le Pollet, St Peter Port
☎ 730844

Live Music

The Doghouse
The Rohais, St Peter Port
☎ 721302

Newspapers

The Guernsey Evening Press and Star – published daily
The Guernsey Globe – published weekly.

Pets

There are no restrictions on animals arriving from the UK or from any other Channel Island, but if you bring your pet, don't take it on any day trip to France without a pet passport or it may not be allowed to return without a lengthy period of quarantine. Island authorities are very thorough in enforcing anti-rabies procedures. For further information ☎ 723552.

Places to Visit

NB: Opening times sometimes change: for up to date free information, the Tourist Information Centre on the North Esplanade is always prepared to help visitors with information required.

The Beau Sejour Leisure Centre
Amherst, St Peter Port
☎ 747200
Something here for everyone: ideal for bad weather.

Arts and Crafts

Bruce Russell & Son,
Silversmiths
Le Gron, St Saviour.
☎ 264321
See the largest range of hand-make gold and silverware and jewellery in the Channel Islands. Workshops, cafe, and five acres of landscaped gardens. Open daily, demonstrations at 10:45am each day. Free entry. Free parking.

Catherine Best Studio
The Mill, St Martin's
☎ 237771
Award-winning jewellery designer's collection & studio.
Open Mon–Sat 9.00am–5.30pm and Sun 9.30am-5pm.

Guernsey Candles

Les Petit Capelles, St Sampson

☎ 249686

See candles being made, visit the workshops and giftshop. See the shop which sells only 'feline' items. Open every day throughout the year. 9am–5.30pm. Free entry. Free parking. Buses 5, 5A & 8.

Guernsey Clockmakers

Les Vauxbelets, St Andrew

☎ 236360

See a wide selection of handmade clocks, browse through the giftshop. Open 8.30am –5.30pm Monday to Friday all year, and 10am–4pm each Saturday during the summer season. Free entry. Free parking.

Guernsey Coppercraft

Rocquaine Rd, St Peter Port

☎ 265112

Visit the workshop and showrooms. Open seven days per week Mar–Dec. Free entry. Free parking.

Guernsey Woodcarvers

Les Issues, St Saviour

☎ 265373

Watch the craftsmen at work. Visit the giftshop. Free entry. Free parking.

Moulin Huet Pottery

Rue Moulin Huet, St Martin

☎ 237201

See the potters at work, visit the giftshop for pottery, prints, oil paintings and watercolours. Open 9–5pm Mon–Fri, 10–12.30pm Sun. Bus Route 6/6A, Free parking.

National Trust for Guernsey

26 Cornet Street,
St Peter Port

☎ 728451

Visit the Victorian shop and parlour where sweets come in jars and self-service hasn't been thought of yet! This shop is owned and staffed by the National Trust of Guernsey. Open Tue, Wed, Thur and Sat 10–4pm 27th Mar–mid-Oct.

Oatlands Village

Les Gigands, St Sampson

☎ 244282

See demonstrations of glass blowing, silversmithing and pottery making. Visit the 'decorate it yourself' workshops, and the gift shops. There is a childrens' play area and a cafe. Open 10–5pm. Free parking.

Le Tricoteur

Perelle Bay

☎ 264040

See traditional knitwear being manufactured. Purchase products in the giftshop. Open Mon–Fri 8–5pm. Free Parking.

Museums and Historical Buildings

Brooklands Farm Implement Museum

Kings Mills, Castel

☎ 258422

Bus 5 & 5A. A private museum of old farm implements used in Guernsey over the past 100 years. Open Tue –Sat 9:30am to 4:30pm, Apr–Sep.

Castle Cornet

St Peter Port

☎ 721657

Military and maritime history within a fascinating fortress. Open 10am–5pm Apr–Oct.

Folk Museum

Saumarez Park

☎ 255384

See the collections of domestic Victoriana, old farming equipment, the dairy, the cider barn, and horsedrawn vehicles. Set in beautiful parkland with an adventure playground, tea rooms and National Trust shop. Open 10am–5pm, 20th Mar–Oct.

Fort Grey Shipwreck Museum

Rocquaine Bay

☎ 265036

Illustrating some of the maritime disasters which have occurred in Guernsey waters. Open 10am–5pm Apr–Oct. Free parking.

Hommet Casement Bunker

Fort Hommet Headland, Vazon Bay

☎ 238205

A fully restored German bunker with an original 10.5cm gun. Open Tuesdays, Thursdays and Saturdays 2pm–4pm Apr–Oct inclusive.

German Direction-Finding Tower

Pleinmont Headland

A re-equipped five storey coastal artillery direction finding tower. Open Wed & Sun 2pm –5pm Apr–Nov: Sun Feb–Mar 2pm–4pm (weather permitting)

German Occupation Museum
Behind Forest Parish Church
☎ 238205
Tableaux, video presentations, a life-sized street and artefacts from life in Guernsey, 1940 to 1945. Tea room. Open 10am–5pm. Free parking.

German Underground Military Hospital
La Vassalerie Rd, St Andrew's Parish
☎ 239100
Bus 4/5, 5A. Free parking. The largest military construction in the Channel Islands. Built by slave workers of many nationalities, many of whom died in its construction.
Open daily Sep: 10am–12pm and 2pm–4pm & Oct: 2pm-4pm. Nov: Thursday & Saturdays only – 2pm–3pm.

Guernsey Museum & Art Gallery
St Peter Port
☎ 726518
Tracing the history and exhibiting the art heritage of the Island. Open all year 10am –4pm.

The Little Chapel
Les Vauxbelets, St Andrew.
Open all year, Mon–Sat 9am–5pm, Sun10am –12.30pm.

18th century Loopholed Tower
Rousse Headland
This fully restored tower tells the story of these defence works. Open from 9am each day. Free entry. Free parking.

Sausmarez Manor
St Martins
☎ 235571
Guernsey's only stately home. Main house open Mon–Thu mornings Easter–Oct. Plus afternoons June to September. In the grounds there is a Dolls' House collection. Open daily 10am–5pm and Sun11am–5pm. Closed during Feb, and open only by appointment during Jan.
Also in the grounds, a mini diesel train, childrens' play area, 9 hole pitch and putt, and a wild sub-tropical garden. Open 10am–5pm every day, Easter–Oct. Bus 5, 5A, 6, 6A, 7, 7A, and St Martins Shuttle. Free parking.

St Saviour's Tunnel
Close-by St Saviour's parish church
A complex of tunnels built by the Germans during the occupation. Open 10am–6pm every day May–Sep. Open Tue, Thu, and Sat only during Apr. Free parking.

The Telephone Museum
'Hermes' La Planque, Côbo Rd, Castel
☎ 726518 or 254157
See telephones and switchboards as used in Guernsey since 1896. Open 2pm–5pm Mon–Fri and 7pm–9pm Tue and Wed evenings, Apr–Sep (inclusive). Free entry. Free parking.

La Valette Underground Military Museum
La Valette, St Peter Port
☎ 722300
Visit a German tunnel complex and see a display of Guernsey's military history. Open from 10am–5pm daily.

Victor Hugo's House
Hauteville House, St Peter Port
☎ 721911
Owned by the city of Paris, the house is furnished as Victor Hugo left it. A fascinating insight into the man, his literature, his life and times.

Victoria Tower
Monument Gardens, St Peter Port
Open all year, daily until a half hour before sunset. Keys may be obtained from the Museum & Art Gallery in Candie Gardens. Closed until Spring 2008

Outdoor and Animals
Guernsey Aquarium
Havelet Bay, St Peter Port.
☎ 723301
See colourful fish from many parts of the world. Open 10am to dusk every day.

The Guernsey Freesia Centre
Route Carre, St Sampson.
☎ 248185
See over two acres of freesias under glass. See the picking, bunching and boxing process. Send flowers to friends and family. Free entry.

The Strawberry Farm
Les Issues Vinery, St Saviour.
☎ 264428
Offers a shopping mall, play areas, crazy golf, bumper cars & boats, model railway, café and restaurant.
Open daily. Free entry. Free parking.

Public Holidays

Guernsey celebrates the same public holidays as the UK with the addition of Liberation Day on May 9th.

Sports & Leisure Facilities

Angling and Fishing

You can fish from anywhere on the coastline without needing permission.

Micks Fishing Supplies
Les Canus, St Peter Port
☎ 700390
Can supply all the tackle you need and give you lots of local advice.

Boat Fishing Contacts:

Arnold Brehaut
☎ 263730

Tim Morris
☎ 249524

Dougal Lane (Wreck Fishing)
☎ 727161

Badminton

Beau Sejour Centre
Amherst, St Peter Port
☎ 747200

Bathing Pools

La Vallette, St Peter Port

Clay Pigeon Shooting

Guernsey Clay Pigeon Club
☎ 252212

Cycling

Cycles can be hired from:

Millards, St Peter Port
☎ 720777

Cycleworld
Camp du Roi, Vale
☎ 258285

Electra Car & Bike Hire
North Plantation, St Peter Port
☎ 726926

Flying

Have a trial lesson and see the Island from the air at the same time. Contact: Guernsey Aero Club. ☎ 265254

Golf

Royal Guernsey Golf Club
L'Ancresse Vale
☎ 246523

La Grande Mare, Vazon
☎ 253544

Go Karting

Guernsey Kart Centre
Victoria Avenue, St Sampson
☎ 712666

Horse Riding

Melrose Farm Stables
Rue du Dos d'Ane, Castel
☎ 252151

Le Carrière Stables
Baubigny, St Sampson
☎ 249998

Sub Aqua

Island Divers
☎ 266940

Dive Guernsey
Dive Bunker, Castle Emplacement, St Peter Port
☎ 714525

Sarnia Skin Divers
Castle Emplacement, St Peter Port
☎ 722884

Discover Snorkelling
☎ 249444

Surfing

Freedom
L'Islet Crossroads, St Sampson
☎ 246690

Ten Pin Bowling

The Bowl
Victoria Ave, St Sampson's
☎ 710444

Tennis

Beau Sejour Centre
Amherst, St Peter Port
☎ 747200

King's Leisure Centre
Kings Rd, St Peter Port
☎ 723366

St Martin's Lawn Tennis Club
Rue du Hurel, St Martin
☎ 720203

Walking

Guided walks around Cobo
Silvia Brouard
☎ 254061

Guided Country Walks
Bob Thompson
☎ 263959

Guided walks around St Peter Port
Judy Porter
☎ 256380

Watercolour Painting

Tony Taylor
Greenacre, Rue du Pres St Peter
☎ 264572

Yachting/Sailing

Guernsey Yacht Club
Castle Emplacement, St Peter Port
☎ 722838

Television

Guernsey receives four UK terrestrial channel, and many establishments also pick up French TV.
Satellite TV is also available in the Island. Channel TV serves all the Channel Islands as part of
the IBA network. It provides daily news and weather information as well as occasional features
of local interest.

Tourist Information

Guernsey Information Centre, North Esplanade, St Peter Port. Open seven days per week from
Easter to the end of September Monday to Saturday 9:00am to 5:00pm, and Sunday 10am–1pm.
☎ 01481 723552 mail: enquiries@visitguernsey.com. www.visitguernsey.com

ALDERNEY

Getting there

By Air

Aurigny Air Services operate daily direct scheduled flights from Southampton and Guernsey.
There are connecting flights with Dinard in France, and most British and European Airports via
Guernsey and Jersey. Flight time from Guernsey is approximately 12 minutes. ☎ 822888.
www.aurigny.com Blue Islands Airline also operates a service to Alderney from Southampton,
Guernsey and Jersey. ☎ 727567. www.blueislands.com

By Sea

Sailings throughout the summer from other Channel Islands and France. Contact the Alderney
Tourist Office for details ☎ 823737. www.visitalderney.com

Accommodation

Hotels

Belle Vue
Butes Rd,
☎ 822844
www.bellevue.alderney.com

Harbour Lights
Newtown,
☎ 07781 135 616
www.harbourlightsalderney.com

Rose & Crown
Le Huret,

☎ 823414
The Georgian House,
Victoria St
☎ 822471
www.georgianhousealderney.com

The Victoria
Victoria St
☎ 822754
www.victoriahotelalderney.com

Guest Houses

Aurigny Maison
Longy Rd
☎ 822041

Bonjour Guest House
High St
☎ 822152
www.bonjourguesthouse.co.uk

Chez Nous
Le Venelles
☎ 823633

Farm Court
Le Petit Val
☎ 822075
www.farmcourt-alderney.co.uk

L'Haras
Newtown Rd
☎ 823174
lharas.internet.alderney.gg

Maison Bourgage
☎ 824097
www.maisonbourgage.com

St Anne's
Le Huret
☎ 823145

Simerock
Les Venelles
☎ 823645

Self Catering

Alderney Accommodation
(Agent for a large selection of self-catering properties) ☎ 823332
www.alderney-accommodation.com

There are a number of properties in Alderney which can be let to visitors on a self-catering basis. A complete list may be obtained from the Alderney Tourist Office ☎ 822994

Camping

Saye Campsite
Contact the Warden to check availability of space or fully equipped tent hire.
☎ 822556
camping@alderney.net

Boat trips

Voyager: licensed to carry 12 passengers. Round Island trips take two and a half hours. The boat can also be chartered for trips to France or Herm. Bookings from McAlitser's Fish Shop, Victoria Street, ☎ 823666

Car Hire

Alderney Car Hire (Jeeps & Cars)
☎ 823352

Braye Hire Cars (also Minimokes & Jeeps)
☎ 823881
www.brayehirecars.com

Cycle Hire

Top Gear
☎ 822000

Pedal Power
☎ 822286

Dentist

Dental Practice
Venelles du Milieu
☎ 823131

Hospital

Mignot Memorial Hospital, Crabby. ☎ 822822

Taxi Services

A1 Taxi
☎ 07781 440121

ABC Taxis
☎ 823760

Island Taxis
☎ 823823

JS Taxis
☎ 07781 100830

Useful information and addresses

Alderney Fire Brigade, Crabby ☎ 882672
Alderney Police, St Anne ☎ 882731

SARK

Getting there

The only way to Sark is by sea from one of the other Channel Islands: 45 minutes from Jersey or Guernsey.
A number of companies operate the link. From Guernsey try the Isle of Sark Shipping Company.
☎ 724059 www.sarkshipping.info

Accommodation

Hotels

Aval du Creux
☎ 832036
www.avalducreux.co.uk

La Sablonnerie Hotel
☎ 832061
www.lasablonnerie.com

Stocks
☎ 832001
www.stockshotel.com

Dixcart Hotel
☎ 832015
www.dixcarthotel.com

Hotel Petit Champ
☎ 832046
www.hotelpetitchamp.co.uk

Guest Houses

Beau Sejour
☎ 832034
www.beausejour.co.uk

Maison Pommier Lodge
☎ 832643

Camp sites

La Valette
☎ 832202

Pomme de Chien
☎ 832316

Cycle Hire

Avenue Cycle Hire
The Avenue
☎ 832102

A to B Cycles
☎ 832844
www.atobcycles.sarkpost.com

Places to visit

La Seigneurie Gardens
Open Mon–Sat throughout the season.
☎ 832208
www.laseigneuriegardens.com

HERM

Getting there

By Sea from St Peter Port, Guernsey. Travel Trident Ferry Weighbridge Clock Tower Liberation Monument, St Peter Port ☎ 721379

Accommodation

White House Hotel ☎ 722159 hotel@herm-island.com
Self catering & camping. For details ☎ 722377
For general Information on Herm visit their website www.herm-island.com

Index